Joyful Giving

SERMONS ON
STEWARDSHIP

Edited by
Dan Moseley

Chalice Press

St. Louis, Missouri

Biblical quotations, unless otherwise noted, are from the *New Revised Standard Version Bible*, copyright 1989, Division of Christian Education of the National Council of the Churches of Christ in the USA. Used by permission.

Quotations marked RSV are from the *Revised Standard Version* of the Bible, copyrighted 1946, 1952, © 1971, 1973.

Quotations marked TEV are from the *Good News Bible*–Old Testament: Copyright © American Bible Society 1976. New Testament: Copyright © American Bible Society 1966, 1971, 1976. Used by permission.

Cover Design: Michael Dominguez
Illustration: Bob Watkins

10 9 8 7 6 5 4 3 2 1   97 98 99 00 01 02

Library of Congress Cataloging–in–Publication Data

Moseley, Dan, Editor
   Joyful Giving: Sermons on Stewardship / Dan Moseley, Editor
         p.   cm.
   Includes bibliographical references
   ISBN 0-8272-1711-0
      1. Stewardship, Christians—Sermons. 2. Christian giving—Sermons.
   3. Sermons, American. 4. Christian Church (Disciples of Christ)—Sermons.
   I. Moseley, Dan .
   BV772.J65   1997
   248'.6--dc21

*D*EDICATION

In loving memory of
Cynthia Ranch Moseley
Wife, mother, and companion
April 4, 1941—May 13, 1995

CONTENTS

FOREWORD

The Church Finance Council, in presenting this book of stewardship sermons to the pastors and laity of the Christian Church (Disciples of Christ), is gratified to see increasing interest in all areas of Christian stewardship across the church.

When Robert K. Welsh, Church Finance Council president, met with Disciples pastors to ask how the CFC might help in their ministry, one request many of them made was for a book of sermons on stewardship. This volume is our response to that request.

In accordance with the Church Finance Council commitment to be in partnership with congregations, we invited a local pastor to provide leadership for this project. Dan P. Moseley, senior minister of Vine Street Christian Church, Nashville, Tennessee, graciously accepted our invitation out of his own deep commitment to the church and to the enhancement of the church's discussion about Christian stewardship.

Church Finance Council staff expresses deep appreciation to Dan Moseley for the stewardship of his time and talent in the development of this book, and to those Disciples ministers who have provided these insightful sermons for our use. We commend the sermons to the church as one more tool in the development of all of us as faithful stewards of God's gracious love.

*J*NTRODUCTION

Not again! Not another book of sermons! And on steward-ship, no less! Surely there are more up-to-date topics for a book to cover. You may be right. But let me tell you how this came about and what I thought about it. Then, if it doesn't make sense to buy this book, put it back.

I had the opportunity to visit with Robert Welsh as he was on his way to becoming president of Church Finance Council of the Christian Church (Disciples of Christ). Robert's overriding concern was, "How shall we fund the mission of the church? Where are we going to get the resources for doing the ministry of shar-ing God's love with the world?"

To me as a local pastor, that question had a familiar ring. Along with the lay leadership of my congregation, I ask that ques-tion with some regularity. It struck me that the answer might be hidden somewhere out there in that great field of service called the local congregation. It might be that solutions to the funding of mission are being discovered by those who struggle weekly with proclaiming the liberating word of the gospel.

Theologians are important. Historians are important. But preachers are in the place where the gospel encounters human life daily, and they just might be finding fresh and creative ways to undergird the mission of the church into the twenty-first cen-tury. So I decided to find out what was out there.

I wrote a list of pastors whom I know and asked them to send me a couple of sermons on the topic of stewardship for pos-sible inclusion in a book. We advertised our request for sermons in publications of the church. We wrote all the regional ministers asking for names of persons who were considered good preach-ers. (My assumption is that much good preaching is going on in small, out-of-the-way places by people who are not well known.) We wrote Disciples homiletics professors and asked them for a sermon or two. We reviewed all the sermons that were presented in Church Finance Council mailings to determine if some were worth adding to such a book. After several months, I ended up with one hundred fifty sermons!

Then the work really began. I read all the sermons to deter-mine whether they helped me understand how modern persons can manage our resources in such a way as to reflect obedience to God. I narrowed the original group down to seventy-five and read those again. Finally, sermons were selected for this collection on the basis of several criteria.

•Are they theologically sound? That is, do they reflect understandings of the God of biblical faith and human encounters with that God?

•Are they fresh in their approach? There are many good approaches to stewardship, but we are preaching to a new generation. The pre–World War II people who make up the majority of our present mainline congregations operate from a different set of fundamental understandings than do those born afterward. Much that has been written about giving in the church speaks in the language of duty and loyalty, language that doesn't resonate well with younger people. I sought to determine whether there were new approaches that could effectively communicate with this generation.

•Are there good stories that others can use? So many times the stories in sermons are old and well worn. That doesn't mean they're bad. It simply means that they are already available in other sources. I was looking for stories that might not be as familiar so that present-day preachers could discover new insights to share.

•Does the sermon deal with one of several areas of management of resources? We certainly help in dealing with money, and this focus prevails here. But some sermons deal with our management of environmental resources, and the management of the institutions that serve others.

I wish to thank the following people for their encouragement and assistance: Cindy Moseley, my wife who believed in me, who died while this project was underway; Robert Welsh, friend and colleague who encourages me; Narka Ryan, colleague and collaborator who worked with me to collect and evaluate these sermons; Gloria Gaskins, executive secretary of Vine Street Christian Church, for her hours of work in communicating and typing; Donna Russell, administrative assistant in the Church Finance Council, for her computer entry of the sermons.

I also offer a special word of gratitude to all the clergy who submitted sermons to me, including those not represented here. I am grateful to the laity of the congregations who have been served by all these preachers. The hunger of the laity brings out offerings from the clergy. The faithful living of the laity makes strong congregations that are the sources of the stories and sermons that you hold in your hands.

May this offering of ideas stimulate and challenge you and your congregation.

Dan Moseley

$\mathcal{M}$AY I GIVE MYSELF AGAIN?

C. William Nichols

> *Well-crafted stories have profound impact. They cling to*
> *the heart's memory and continue to nourish the soul.*
> *This sermon has several stories that reflect the growing*
> *devotion people have to that which is precious to them.*
> *Tell these stories in your own sermons.*

Romans 12:1–8

Ceremonial occasions have a way of calling for speeches, and golden wedding anniversary celebrations are no exception. Usually, the husband and wife being honored on such an occasion are called upon to say a few words to the assorted guests who are standing around, trying not to look too uncomfortable, balancing the crystal cup on the crystal plate with the cake and nuts and mints. The standard jokes are told, the husband and wife are taking playful jabs at each other, wondering aloud how they could have managed to put up with each other for such a jaw-gaping span of years.

The husband and wife look scrubbed and shining for their big moment. She wears an orchid corsage on her left shoulder—quite possibly the first time in her life she has received such an extravagant floral offering. The children and grandchildren are gathered around them as they cut the decorated cake. Then, in reply to the friendly urging of their guests to make some remarks, Slim kisses his wife Betty on the cheek, squeezes her hand gently, and moves to the microphone.

Slim is not known for his speech-making ability. He is a quiet, stocky, hard-working man. He stands silently for a

Bill Nichols is retired in Decatur, Illinois, after an extended period as senior pastor of Central Christian Church there. He served as interim general minister and president of the Christian Church (Disciples of Christ) in 1991-93.

1

moment, staring at the microphone. Then he lifts his eyes toward the gathered friends and neighbors, offers a simple, sincere thanks to his family and friends, and relates a story he has read somewhere.

"When Victoria was queen of the British Empire," he begins, "she once visited the Punjab in India. Her empire stretched around the globe. Britain ruled the seas. When Queen Victoria spoke, the world listened. That afternoon in the Punjab, she was told that a young prince of a minor province would like to make a presentation to her. She said, 'Show him in.'

"The young prince—really just a small child—knelt before the queen. Then he stood, reached into his pocket, and held out a small cloth bag. The queen's attendant opened the bag. A large, brilliant, polished diamond fell into his hand. The audience gasped a little, each one whispering to the other about the gigantic size of the stone. Queen Victoria thanked the child-prince and promised him that his generous gift would become a permanent part of the royal treasury of crown jewels in London.

"Many years later, the young prince made a trip to England. He asked to see the aging Queen Victoria. She was reminded of the young man's earlier gift and granted him an audience. After the proper introductions were made, the young man asked if he might see the diamond he had given to the queen many years before. It was brought from the vault and handed to him. 'Your Highness,' he said, 'Years ago when I was a small child, I gave this diamond to you. At that time I had no idea how much this stone was worth. Now I am a man. Now I know how much this stone is really worth. May I give it to you again, with all my heart?'"

Slim pauses and turns toward Betty. "I am not a fancy stone," he says. "Nobody would give many dollars for this weathered body. Once I stood at the altar of our church and gave myself to you in marriage. Like that young child-prince giving his priceless gift, I did not really know at that time what I was giving you. But now, after fifty years, the Great Depression, a World War, a chorus of laughter and an ocean of tears, much hard work and countless prayers, two wonderful kids, beautiful grandchildren, and a lot of scrambled eggs and bologna sandwiches, I know how much this life means to me. Betty, now that I know what it's worth, may I give myself to you again—with all my heart?"

I wonder if that isn't similar to the testimony every one of you could make about your own commitments. When you said your "I do's" in a marriage ceremony, or when you accepted employment and contracted with your employer to give your best work, or when you took your membership vows in some organization, you couldn't see into the future, to know beyond all doubt what that commitment would cost you. But at every point along the way, as you encountered the unexpected demands, you gave yourself again in fresh commitments that represented not only your continuing faith but your continuing willingness—in various unforeseen circumstances—to confirm your commitment in faithful performance.

Everyone who belongs to the church once made a confession of faith, in which you gave yourself to the Lordship of Jesus Christ. You accepted the sovereignty of his rule over your life. You didn't know at the time what that commitment might cost you in all the years to come. And sadly, there are many people who later turn back from the commitment. They abrogate their vows of Christian discipleship; they resign from being Christian when they find that it costs more of them than they want to give.

A young man came to his pastor for counsel on how much he should give to his church. The pastor carefully showed him, through a study of scriptures, that the tithe is the divinely prescribed standard for giving—ten percent of one's income returned to God through his church. The young man promised God to be a tither. At that time, in his first joy, he was making $50 a week, so he faithfully brought his $5 tithe to church every Sunday. But the Lord blessed his with growing prosperity. Soon he was making $100 a week (of which he gave his tithe of $10). Then, because he was diligent and creative and effective in his work, he continued to be promoted until he was making $200, then $300; and still he tithed regularly.

Finally one day he came back to his pastor with a complaint. "Pastor," he said, "when I promised God I would tithe, I was only making $50 a week, and it wasn't too hard to tithe my $5. And it wasn't so serious when I made $100 or $200 a week. But now I'm making $500. And the tithe on that is $50 a week. I don't see how I can possibly give that much. Can you do something to release me from that promise I made to God?"

The pastor replied, "Well, I really don't have the authority to release you from a promise you made to God. But I'll tell you what I will do. I will pray that God will reduce your income to make it easier for you to tithe."

Every time you make a pledge to God through the church, every time you put your tithe into the offering plate, you are reconfirming your confession of faith, renewing the commitment you once made to God; you are offering evidence that you have not reneged on the promise you made to him when you and God pledged yourselves to each other, to walk through life together and to share each other's concerns and fill each other's needs. When you make a pledge, you are saying to God, "Now that I know what life is all about, now that I know what commitment costs, may I give myself to You again?"

This year in our stewardship campaign, we are seeking two kinds of commitments from our members: their estimate of giving for the general fund, and a three-year commitment of giving for capital funds to provide additional facilities for our growing congregation. The good news is that both of these aspects of our stewardship campaign are healthy symptoms of a church that is growing and laying the necessary foundations for a future that will be our most glorious chapter. Sacrifice is called for, as we consider both of these opportunities for commitment. A love that is not willing to sacrifice is not love at all.

One day a group of men—all about the same age—were discussing how much it costs to bring up children. They were complaining about the cost of school and college, and clothes and music lessons, and medical care and allowance.

One man, who had listened but not entered into the conversation, said: "Many years ago God sent us a little baby girl. We promised to be the best parents we could possibly be, but we had no idea how much it would cost. And the older she got, the more expensive she was. Braces on her teeth, ballet and piano lessons, all the latest fads in clothes so that she could dress like all her friends. It kept my pockets empty just raising that daughter. Then she went away to college and the costs multiplied: tuition, books, a car to drive, dues to her sorority, boarding costs. Oh, yes, I complained about it a lot.

"Then, one night we received a telephone call informing us that our daughter had died in an automobile accident. And you know, she hasn't cost us a cent since that time."

I suppose we all have to learn through practical—and sometimes painful—experience that what we love we have to keep paying for. Our love requires a commitment that demands of us some continuing evidence of our priorities.

But strengthening us in this commitment is the presence of a living Christ who not only showed his love and commitment by giving his life on the cross but who continues to come to us every day that we live, offering to let his presence be the power we need to live victoriously. Every day he says to us, "May I give myself to you again?" And it is no less than this that the Christ asks of us. Will you give yourself to him again? Now that you know what commitment costs, will you give yourself to him again—and with all your heart?

$\mathcal{T}$HE GRACE OF GIVING

Cynthia L. Hale

> *This is an excellent example of a biblically outlined presentation. The people in Corinth become models for the people in churches today. The need of the mother church becomes the motivating force for grace-filled giving. It grows out of a sense of belonging to God and therefore a belonging to each other. This sermon invites the listener to respond to the needs of brothers and sisters because of our love for the One who creates us as one family.*

2 Corinthians 8:1–7

The apostle Paul was on a mission. The successful evangelist, church planter, theologian and pastor was now trying something new: fund-raising. His cause was the alleviation of poverty among the members of the First Christian Church in Jerusalem. The brothers and sisters were in financial trouble. They needed help.

The mother ship was shipwrecked. The church born on Pentecost that had experienced a wonderful time of fullness was now experiencing want.

It can happen to anyone. Some of us know that firsthand. One minute you're up, the next you're down. One minute you are experiencing showers of blessing, the next all hell breaks loose.

If perchance you haven't been through a storm in your life yet—just wait! Your time is coming. Into each life some rain will fall. It's inevitable. It's a given. It is the nature of life. It is a fact of life. Life can be rough!

Storms are also a given in the life of a Christian. If you thought that by becoming a Christian you would never experience any more hard times, you've got another thought coming.

Jesus himself said, "In the world you have tribulation; but be of good cheer, I have overcome the world" (John 16:33, RSV).

Cynthia Hale is founding pastor of the Ray of Hope Christian Church in Decatur, Georgia, and a recent first vice moderator of the Christian Church (Disciples of Christ).

In this world, it's not "you might...." You *will* have troubles. You *will* have difficulties. You *will* be disappointed. You *will* be rejected. You *will* be talked about, lied about—you will be. But be of good cheer—Jesus has overcome the world.

In Christ, we are overcomers. In Christ, we have the victory. When you go through the waters, God will be with you. When you pass through the rivers, they will not overtake you. When you go through the fire, you will not be burned (see Isaiah 43:2). Nevertheless, you must go through!

The Jerusalem Christians were going through hard times, and they needed help. So Paul decided to give leadership to a campaign among the Gentile Christians to provide aid to their brothers and sisters in Jerusalem.

It is this issue that he is addressing in this letter to the Corinthians. A year earlier, in his first letter, Paul had asked for their help, as we see recorded in 1 Corinthians 16:1–3:

> Now concerning the collection for the saints: you should follow the directions I gave to the churches of Galatia. On the first day of every week, each of you is to put aside and save whatever extra you earn, so that collections need not be taken when I come. And when I arrive, I will send any whom you approve with my letters to take your gift to Jerusalem.

The collection for God's people that Paul was referring to was the special offering to help the brothers and sisters in Jerusalem. He wrote to all the Gentile churches making a special appeal because the folks were in need.

The Jerusalem Christians' need provided their sisters and brothers in Christ an opportunity to express unity and solidarity with them. It also provided the Gentile churches an occasion to do ministry beyond their local situation, meeting the needs of others in a tangible and concrete way.

This is what it means to be Christian. We belong to one another, and we are to have equal concern for each other. If one suffers, we all suffer. We are to care for and take care of one another. I can't make it without you, and you can't make it without me.

No matter how independent and self-sufficient we may feel and want to believe that we are, it's not so. Persons who live alone and secluded from everyone else can never fully develop and become the persons that God created them to be. We were created for relationship with God and one another. Someone penned,

> No one is an island,
> No one stands alone.

Each one's joy is joy to me,
Each one's pain is my own.
We need one another, so I will defend.
Each one as my brother, my sister.
Each one as my friend.

We do need one another, not just inside the walls of the church, but beyond. Those of us who have entered the fellowship of believers are within the ark of safety, but many others are not. Many of us have; many have not. We are blessed; many are not. The world is filled with hurting, hungry persons who are not looking for a handout. They need a hand. They are looking for someone who cares, someone who would dare to make that caring real.

When the Corinthians heard about the need of the Jerusalem church, they eagerly responded and pledged their support. But when collection time came, they failed to show up for the showdown. They did not follow through. In other words, they didn't send the money.

We aren't sure why. Someone said that it might have had something to do with their strained relationships with Paul. They had a disagreement with him because he had to discipline them. Though the Corinthians were quite gifted, they were also quite immature in their faith; or at least they were acting like it.

I know this isn't true of any of you, but some folks, when they get mad or dissatisfied with the pastor or the program, refuse to give to the church. I know none of you would do that. You wouldn't let a disagreement with anyone keep you from blessing God and God's people through you.

We really don't know why the Corinthians didn't give. But it sure wasn't because they didn't have it. The Corinthians weren't rich, but they weren't poor either. They just had not given yet, and Paul was concerned. He wrote to tell them so. He wanted them to complete this act of grace on their part.

Didn't they realize that their giving was an indication of their spirituality and their maturity in Christ? They were a gifted church, excelling in everything else, and so Paul said, "just as you excel in everything—in faith, in speech, in knowledge, in complete earnestness and in your love for us—see that you also excel in this grace of giving" (2 Corinthians 8:7).

Paul's method of maturing the Corinthians was to brag to them and give them an example of a group of churches who had excelled in this giving under extremely difficult circumstances. The Macedonian churches had given liberally to the cause as an act of grace, motivated, enabled by the grace of God in their lives. Paul makes that clear in verse 1:

> And now brothers and sisters, we want you to know about the grace that God has given the Macedonian Church. Out of the most severe trial, their overwhelming joy and their extreme poverty welled up in rich generosity. For I testify that they gave as much as they were able and even beyond their ability.

The Macedonian Church had heard about the opportunity to help their brothers and sisters in Jerusalem who were going through difficult times, and they gave generously. But notice that they, too, were having their difficulties.

Paul says they were going through the most severe trial and experiencing extreme poverty. The Greek word used here for extreme poverty refers to a "beggar who has nothing and nowhere to get anything." They needed someone to help them—somebody needed to take up a collection for *them*.

And if the truth be told—and you know that I am about telling the truth, the whole truth and nothing but the truth—that is what many of us use as an excuse for not giving. We are fond of saying, "I ain't got nothing to give. I'm broke. I can't help myself right now, much less someone else. And when I go to church looking for some relief, all I hear is that I need to help someone else. Give me a break! I don't have it! You can't get blood out of a turnip, can you?"

That's true, and you cannot force anyone to give who does not have it or who does not want to give. But listen to this. Even though the Macedonian Christians were going through their own trials and were experiencing poverty, they gave. They didn't just give; they gave generously. They gave as much as they were able and beyond their ability. Their giving was an act of grace, in response to grace.

"Grace," as you know, comes from the Greek word *charis*. It is the freely given, undeserved favor and forgiveness that God offers through Jesus Christ to those who accept it by faith. "We are saved by grace through faith," a gift of God, not by our own achievement or works that we can boast about.

Grace is also divine enablement, the ability to do that which we in our own strength alone cannot do. When we are weak, God is sufficient. When we are running short, the grace of God makes up the difference. When we cannot see our way, it is grace that carries us safely through.

God's grace is sufficient for every need and work. Paul reminds us in Philippians 2:12–13 that while we are to work out our salvation with fear and trembling, God is at work in us, both to will and to act according to God's good purpose.

Paul said that the Macedonian churches, in their most severe trial, when they were at their lowest, when they couldn't see their way clear, by God's grace their overwhelming joy and their extreme poverty welled up in rich generosity.

Now I want you to take note of two sets of contrasts given here: heavy affliction and abundant joy, extreme poverty and rich generosity. Now from a human perspective, there is no way that heavy affliction and overflowing joy or extreme poverty and rich generosity could have anything in common.

But from God's perspective, as made clear in scripture, joy is not freedom from outward difficulty. Joy is the overcoming of difficulties that faith gives. Joy is not the absence of hard times, poverty, sickness, sorrow, or trouble in your life. Rather, it is the presence of God. Joy comes in knowing that no matter what is going on in our lives, God is able.

While joy is the fruit of the Spirit, we must make a conscious effort to claim joy. We must claim the presence of joy in our lives. But the other thing we must realize is that the capacity for great joy, overflowing joy, is developed in us through great difficulty. The greater the trial, the greater the capacity for joy within.

A couple of years ago, I was going through a difficult time. The pain was so deep that it felt like no human hand could soothe it. I kept rubbing my heart trying to get some relief. But I couldn't reach the pain. I called out to God for relief, and God said that I needed to go through. The pain, God said, is digging a well in you that I will soon fill with my joy.

The trials that I was going through were laying a foundation for overflowing joy. That's the way it was with the Macedonians. Furthermore, God used the difficulties to mold and shape them in God's will. Through what they were experiencing, they discovered the reality of God's love and power. They began to really trust and depend on God rather than their own ability.

Isn't that what Andre Crouch was talking about when he said:

> If I never had a problem I wouldn't know that God
> could solve them. I wouldn't know what faith in God
> could do. Through it all, through it all, I've learned
> to trust in Jesus. I've learned to trust in God. Through
> it all, through it all, I've learned to depend upon God's
> word.

Through their poverty, the Macedonians were released from the control that money can often have on us. When you have money, you think you've got it all together. Money makes us proud; money makes us feel self-sufficient. Money makes us think that it is because of who we are rather than whose we are that we have what we have. Money causes us to forget who and whose we are. We forget that if it had not been for God's grace, as Paul says in verse 9,

> For you know the grace of our Lord Jesus Christ that
> though he was rich, yet for your sakes he became poor
> so that through his poverty, we might become rich.

Jesus gave us the supreme example of giving and grace when he left glory and took on our humanity. When we consider God's grace and Christ's gift of himself, how can we give anything less?

Through their poverty, the Macedonians gave. Their poverty no more impeded their generosity than their afflictions diminished their joy. They realized that you have to make a choice to have joy.

Giving is an act of grace. It is God who gives the resources and then opens the hands of those who want to give.

Now the question that each of us must ask is whether or not this grace of giving has been created in us. How can we know? When we give as an act of grace:

(1) We give in spite of our difficulties. Circumstances do not determine nor do they diminish our giving. We are consistent in our giving no matter who happens in our lives.

(2) We give willingly. The Macedonians did not have to be prompted or reminded constantly to give. As a matter of fact, they asked for the privilege of giving.

(3) We give sacrificially. David said, "I will not offer burnt offerings to the LORD my God that cost me nothing." (2 Samuel 24:24.)

The key to all of this is that the Macedonians first gave themselves to the Lord, and that's what motivated them to give so freely to others.

The story is told of a missionary who presented the gospel to a wealthy Indian chief. The chief in response tried to give the missionary cattle, land, and other things that the chief owned, to which the missionary responded: "God doesn't want your things.

God wants you." The chief replied, "Your God is a very wise God. For God knows that once God has the chief, God has the cattle, the land, and everything the chief owns."

All God wants is you. Once God has you, everything else follows.

WHAT GAVE GIVING A BAD NAME?

David A. Shirey

Why is giving a four-letter word for so many of us? This sermon explores the negative attitudes toward giving and points to faith issues that change that. As pastors, we experience resistance. This sermon helps work it through so that people can discover joy in giving.

2 Corinthians 8:1–7

A poll was taken among preachers. The question was, "What is your least favorite part of the ministry?" What do you think the top response was? The most-mentioned least favorite was the annual stewardship campaign. I can't help but believe that if a similar poll were to be taken among the laity, the response would be the same. I suspect that one of the least-anticipated events on the church calendar is the annual stewardship campaign. Like preacher, like congregation. Think of that: inviting persons to give to the cause of Jesus Christ by pledging a portion of their money to his church is one of the least favorite things that preachers and members of their congregations do in a year. All of which raises this simple question: What gave giving a bad name?

Well, I've given that question some thought and I'm prepared to put forth what I think gave giving such a bad name.

For starters, it strikes me that giving doesn't come naturally to us. There is something deep down inside us that makes us against giving from the start. I say that because I can't help but notice that when I put my finger in my four-month-old daughter's open palm, she grasps it and holds on to it and will not let go, as if maybe we're born with the inclination to grasp and hold on to things. And I can't help but notice that my

---

David Shirey is senior minister of First Christian Church in Wilmington, North Carolina.

four-year-old has become quite adept at calling out the names of the holy trinity at the top of her lungs. Not Father, Son, and Holy Spirit, mind you, but rather "Me! My! Mine!" as if she were born with those words in her vocabulary. And I can't help but remember the exchange that my wife and I engaged in prior to our move from St. Louis four years ago, exactly the same exchange we had four years before that when moving from Nashville. Looking out over our belongings, I said, "Where on earth did we get all this stuff?" She replied, "Well, what do *you* want to get rid of?" and I replied, "Well, some of *your* stuff. I *need* all my stuff."

In that moment, I felt like an old magnet I found one day in a desk drawer, coated with paper clips, pins, and every metal do-dad imaginable. Is there something within me that attracts, accumulates, and holds on to, but never lets go of, anything that comes within my sphere of influence? It seems as if grasping; "me! my! mine-ing!"; hoarding; and never letting go are what come naturally to human beings. It's giving, sharing, and letting go that go against the grain. That would explain why the annual stewardship campaign is a perennial least-favorite thing, why it's greeted with such groans ("Here they go again!"), why it's tolerated with such grudging spirits, and why pen is put to pledge card with such painful reluctance. It seems giving is contrary to human nature. It rubs us the wrong way. So maybe it's human nature that gave giving a bad name.

But there's more to it than that. There's also the notion, deep-seated in all of us, that we don't have a whole lot *to* give. We've convinced ourselves that we really don't have much. How can we give when we're barely getting by on what we have? This brings to mind a poll that was done a few years back. The question was asked, "How much *more* would you need to make in order to be more secure?" The answer was, "About 20 percent more than I make now." Regardless of whether the person interviewed made $15,000 or $115,000, the answer was the same—I need 20 percent more. This tells me that if we've convinced ourselves that we simply don't have anything *to* give (given the little we have), then no wonder the annual stewardship campaign is among our least-favorite things. It's asking us to do what we really can't do. How can we be expected to give away something when we don't have enough in the first place? So, maybe that's what gave giving a bad name.

On the other hand, maybe giving got its bad name from some of the abuses we've seen in the past few years. You know what I mean—the TV evangelists and their air-conditioned dog houses. It has come to the point that when I stand up in the pulpit and mention money, you probably envision a toll-free number parading across the screen right under my chin. You hear me mention giving and you subconsciously push the mute button—"Oh boy, here he goes again. Where there's a preacher, there's an offering plate not far behind." Maybe that's why the stewardship campaign is listed as least favorite on so many ballots. "All they talk about is money and then look how they use what they get!" So maybe that's what gave giving a bad name.

Or maybe it's a combination of all of the above that gave giving a bad name. In the first place, it's against our nature *to* give, so it rubs us the wrong way when we're asked. What's more, we don't have enough as it is, and even if we did, "Who you gonna trust these days to give it to?"

Having said all that, what do you make of this? I know some folks who gave giving a *good* name! I have discovered in my research a pastor and a congregation for whom the annual stewardship campaign was not something to be dreaded and endured, but rather something to be done with a spirit of expectation and joy. I have to tell you, brothers and sisters, about the grace of God which was shown in the churches of Macedonia. For in a severe test of affliction, their abundance of joy and their extreme poverty overflowed in a wealth of liberality on their part. They gave according to their means, as I can testify, and beyond their means, of their own free will, even begging for the favor of taking part in the campaign!

You heard me right: a congregation that actually *begged* for the favor of giving! I have it all right here in black and white in a letter from their preacher, a fellow by the name of Paul. What do you make of this? In all my years in the church, I've never seen anything like it before. Contrary to human nature, they begged for the favor of being invited to give. Contrary to the reluctance you and I are familiar with, their giving was accompanied by an abundance of joy—they were downright *cheerful* givers. If that were not enough, these folks really didn't have enough. They were truly poor. But surprise, surprise—out of their extreme poverty there overflowed a wealth of liberality. They gave according to their means and beyond. Beats anything I've ever seen. These folks gave giving a *good* name.

Now this got me to wondering. I asked myself, "How'd they do it?" I mean, with all there is to give giving a bad name and with the way most churches and preachers enter into the annual stewardship campaign kicking and screaming, what did they do differently?

According to their preacher, Paul, there *was* a turning point all right. There was a point when, for those people and that preacher, "give" ceased being a four-letter word and became something they took great pleasure in doing. What was the turning point? "First, they gave themselves to the Lord...." They took Jesus Christ as their Lord and Savior and pledged to love the Lord their God with all their heart and all their soul and their might. Having done that, all their treasure followed, and joyfully at that! Which is to say that when a congregation and pastor give themselves first to the Lord, it makes all the difference in the world. Hearts are warmed, attitudes are changed, and human nature is transformed. In other words, giving is given a good name. When people truly give themselves to the Lord, hands that before held, grasped, and hoarded, find themselves finally able to open up, let go, and give. Voices that before growled "Mine!" find themselves finally able to say "Thine!" When people truly give themselves to the Lord first, hearts are filled to overflowing with the unspeakable riches of God's grace to the point that I *know* I am rich and so I *want* to give to the One from whom all blessings flow.

Do you know that it still happens today? When people give themselves first to the Lord, heart, might, mind, and soul, giving is given a good name. Extraordinary things happen. Spirits soar. Pledges are made with reverent pleasure. Yes, it still happens today. I went to a church one day last year, went into worship, and wouldn't you know, I happened to be there on the very Sunday they were doing their stewardship campaign. I must admit, I rolled my eyes and said, "Oh boy." They had some preacher there who launched into some stewardship thing and then they passed out pledge cards and I took one just because everybody else did and I sat there all uncomfortable. (You see, giving had been given such a bad name in my book.) But then something happened I'll never forget. As I sat there in this church, pledge card in hand...as I sat there in *this* church, pledge card in hand, I lifted my eyes and saw the people in this church give what I could tell was prayerful attention to their cards. Then, as I watched, you stepped out of the pews, came down the aisle, and put your cards in the silver bowl in front of the communion table. As you did, I noticed a look of worshipful reverence in your eyes—you looked like I thought you must have looked when you first came down the aisle to make your confession of faith those many years ago. Then it dawned on me, that's exactly what you folks in this church were doing. Sure enough, you were giving yourselves first to the Lord, giving yourselves again, giving yourselves gladly, and your giving gladly followed. Then I watched as the people in this church made their way back to the fellowship hall for dinner. When the report was finally read and so many had given out of their own means and even beyond with an overflowing of liberality, one of our long-time members came up to me and with wide-eyed amazement said, "Well, that beats anything I've ever seen!" I didn't ask her to explain. I understood. She was experiencing the same thrill Paul had experienced. It is the thrill that comes when people give of themselves first to the Lord, the thrill that comes when Christians give giving a *good* name.

ℋOW MUCH IS ENOUGH?

Gilbert D. Davis, Jr.

This sermon is down-to-earth and practical. It deals with the questions ministers are regularly asked. It recognizes the motivation to give at two levels—from others and from ourselves. With many people coming to church who have no training in Christian living, simple, practical, didactic sermons like this are in great demand.

"Before the month ends, every member of this congregation will have the opportunity to make a pledge of financial support to the work of Christ through his church." That kind of announcement, to many people, is about as exhilarating as a dust storm. In most Disciples congregations, some kind of every-member financial commitment program is undertaken each year. Many regard these stewardship campaigns as essential but routine. What could be more commonplace than making another church pledge?

This year we intend to lift the process of Christian pledging above the ordinary. We are able to do that in other matters. For example, each Sunday we gather about the Lord's table and take from it a little piece of bread and a little cup of wine, common items. In this household of faith, however, these ordinary objects stand for more than themselves. They are the outward and visible sign of what we most profoundly believe.

It is my prayer that, when we come to the climax of this stewardship emphasis and each of us holds in his or her hands a simple card and a pencil, these everyday articles will take on a sacramental character.

A simple commitment card could become the outward and visible sign of the new commitment of our lives to Jesus Christ.

Gilbert Davis stays active in retirement in Fort Worth, Texas, after an extended period as director of church relations for Texas Christian University.

If that happens, Consecration Day will be a good day for each of us and a good day for this church.

Think with me about practical answers to two questions: Why do Christians give? How much is enough?

I. Why do Christians Give?

The obvious answer for many church members is that the church needs money. Beyond a doubt, the church does need money to extend the life, the love, and the saving influence of Jesus Christ. Recently, for example, the Commission on Finance of the Christian Church (Disciples of Christ) had to notify units to expect smaller appropriations in the coming years.

Current budget cuts for the Division of Overseas Ministries mean that Donna Wisehart, who works in health care all over the island of Jamaica, will continue doing her work without a car. Felix Ortiz, who is training lay pastors in Paraguay, will be eight-to-ten thousand dollars short of what is needed to get that program through the year. Ludhiana Hospital in Punjab, India, the only medical facility comparable to American hospitals, will sink further into debt.

Reduced allocations to the National Benevolent Association will mean that an additional, desperately needed facility to care for abused children cannot be provided at this time.

For the same reason, the Southwest region will not be able to assist deserving pastors to enroll in programs of continuing education.

Let us acknowledge, without hesitation, that the church does need money—a great deal more than it is getting. But there is a more important reason why Christians ought to provide financial resources for the church's mission: that is *the need of the giver to give*.

I once served as pastor of a congregation that moved to a new location, necessitating dramatic increases in contributions by its members. After several years of making building payments, the church board chairman voiced the attitude of many in the church, saying, "Since the mortgage is paid, we won't have to give as much as we did." As pastor, I was distressed because many of those people had grown in the Christian life in more ways than the size of their gifts during the years of increased giving.

Visiting with a veteran minister, I voiced my alarm over the anticipated decline in giving based on the congregation's diminishing need for funds. He said to me, "You have been asking your people to give for the wrong reason. If I ask you to give to meet my needs, then I am a beggar." Often the church has assumed the role of a beggar in order to fund the mission to which Christ has called us.

The truth is that the church will not be plunged into bankruptcy because you and I do not give or serve. Jesus said, "I will build my church and the gates of hell shall not prevail against it." (Matthew 16:18, KJV.) The effect of closefisted giving is far more devastating to the individual who practices it than to the church. Someone has stated the matter succinctly: "Token giving is spiritual suicide."

The greatest need in my life and yours is the need to give ourselves to God through Jesus Christ. Christianity is not a gimmick but an altar. God cannot fully give to us until we begin to give ourselves to God, and this we cannot do without giving our money. Jesus said, "Where your treasure is, there your heart will be also." (Matthew 6:21.)

II. How Much is Enough?

Most of us are uncertain about this question: "How much is enough?" I am not so brash as to tell you that I know precisely what you ought to give. The truth of the matter is that I have not plumbed the depths of that question for myself.

As a student in Brite Divinity School, I was leaving a classroom one day when a distinguished, gray-haired gentleman approached me. He extended his hand and said, "My name is Arthur A. Everts." He asked if I was studying to be a minister. I responded affirmatively, and he continued, "I would like to visit with you about a very important matter." I did not know then that Mr. Everts was the proprietor of the largest jewelry store west of the Mississippi River or that East Dallas Christian Church was born in his living room. It was my assumption that he was some kind of fanatic, and I would have preferred to escape from him. He was kind but persistent.

In a few moments I found myself in a classroom with the door shut, and this devout layman preached me a sermon on tithing. It was the first message I had heard that presented tithing in a favorable light. It made me uncomfortable. I was irritated by Mr. Everts' words. He ended his sermon by extending an invitation for me personally to become a tither—right on the spot.

My response was made with a feeling of righteous indignation: "Mr. Everts, we are not living under law but under grace." With a twinkle in his eye he replied, "Young man, you are just as right as you can be, but if you can find any words in the New Testament that say less is expected of Christians living under grace than was required of Jewish people living under the law, I will be glad to join you in that proposition."

I didn't have a good argument then, and I don't now. But like the rich young ruler, I went away sorrowful. However, that old gentleman planted a seed in my life that grew until ultimately I came to see the tithe not as a hampering legalism but as a means of grace.

My wife and I didn't, for a moment, believe that when we became tithers we had reached the ultimate in Christian giving. In fact, we said to each other, "If we can tithe on the small income we have now, when we get better off, we'll do better." We did get better off financially, but we didn't give a larger percent of our income until, in a Consecration Day effort, an effective guest leader challenged us to take a step beyond the tithe. We have not arrived as stewards of our possessions. We still have a long way to go.

I don't know where you are, but I know enough about church members to know that all of us are in one of three places. Some of us are at the very beginning of our pilgrimage as Christian stewards. It would be a wonderful thing for some here today to decide to become percentage givers.

A good starting place is half a tithe, or five percent, which is one dollar per week per thousand dollars of annual income. Then make a covenant with God to grow each year until you reach the tithe.

This may be the time when several of our members will step up to the tithe (which is two dollars per week per thousand dollars of annual income). Others of us began giving a tenth when we had less and loved less than we do now. We never believed that tithing was the ceiling but the floor. It is a place to begin rather than a place to stop. It is our prayer that whatever financial commitment you make as individuals and families, it will represent growth, and that each of us will grow one step or at least one percent this year.

How long has it been since you felt you truly belonged to God because, through a conscious act, you gave yourself?

That is what Consecration Day or Pledge Sunday is all about. In the near future, you will hold a pledge card and a pencil in your hand. In this family of faith, it is hoped that what you will be dealing with is more than paper and pencil. That card could be the outward and visible sign of the new commitment of your life to Jesus Christ.

$\mathcal{B}$EYOND OUR EXPECTATIONS

G. Hugh Wilson

> *To preach weekly to a continuous community of faith*
> *requires the preacher to be a pastor. We who are pastors*
> *know that the persons in the pew are diverse—each in a*
> *different place. This sermon recognizes that, and seeks to*
> *address each person with a needed word about*
> *the management of his or her resources.*

Ephesians 3:14–21

A man was hunting in the forest when a storm came up. Looking for shelter from the rain, he found and crawled into a hollow log, which fitted quite snugly. The rain lasted for hours and soaked the wood. When the storm was over, the hunter was unable to get out. He was held tight. Finally exhausted, he gave up, knowing he would starve to death. His life flashed before him. When he remembered the excuses he had given for not practicing Christian stewardship, he felt so small that he was able to crawl out easily!

Many are the reasons we tell such old stories treating a serious and vital subject with humor.

I wish it were possible to bring different messages to different people about Christian stewardship. Trying to challenge and inspire some, we may create guilt for others. Congratulating some, we may induce false complacency among others. Often I would desire three stewardship messages: one for persons new to this congregation, new to the Christian life; one for those whose income and especially their interest has been growing; and one for those whose ability is no longer expanding but who have been consistent and faithful through the years.

The letter to the Ephesians speaks of Christian growth in general, but one expression of our loyalty and our willingness

Hugh Wilson is senior pastor of First Christian Church in Norman, Oklahoma.

to follow Christ is the way we use our money. Stewardship of life includes more than possessions, but it does include money. There are three messages in this passage. Wear the shoe that fits, even if it hurts a little.

I. For the New

First is a message to new members or new Christians: Stewardship is an integral part of being a Christian. "I pray that, according to the riches of his glory, [God] may grant that you may be strengthened in your inner being...and that Christ may dwell in your hearts through faith...." Christian stewardship involves all we do with life. Stewardship is expressed in church attendance. That is only the beginning, but it represents a dedicated use of time. Stewardship is expressed in singing, teaching, sewing, welcoming, and caring, using our talents for God. Stewardship is also expressed in our gifts of money, our use of resources, our financial support, using the ability that God has given us for the purposes and ministries of God.

I want you to know that you belong to an active, committed congregation. Over 350 families and individuals give $370,000 for the expenses of this church and its world outreach effort and another $80,000 for the building fund. Over $450,000 from 350 families represents a strong commitment from a high percentage of our members.

Many of the church of which you are a part are deeply concerned persons who practice a regular discipline of giving, who make significant sacrifices for what they believe to be important. You are surrounded by people who take the church and the claims of God seriously. That is reflected in their stewardship of money. There are enough of us to do significant work, but there are not enough that we can say, "let someone else do it."

Marvin Rannabarger told of his young son, who brought to his attention the Thanksgiving offering box that he had brought home from Sunday School the day before. "Have you put any money in it yet, Dad?" "No, I haven't," Rannabarger replied, "It will have to come from your allowance." "NOT FROM MY ALLOWANCE!" His quick reply ended the discussion. Isn't that typical? We want to fill our offering envelopes or boxes—but not from our allowance (First Christian Church newsletter, Hannibal, Missouri).

What you give is a decision that you and God will make. Your stewardship will be the result of gratitude and a desire to share. There is no coercion, no pressure, no comparison with others that should be allowed to rob you of your decision to be a good steward of possessions, along with all the rest of life. You and your conscience will wrestle with God. When we wrestle, we will give more than anyone would ever dare to ask of us. We hope your stewardship will be an example to the rest of us.

There is a message for the new in our midst.

II. For the Growing

There is also a message to growing Christians: God's cause can be advanced as you reach for new levels, "...that you...being rooted and grounded in love...may have the power to comprehend, with all the saints, what is the breadth and length and height and depth, and to know the love of Christ that surpasses knowledge." We are challenged to reach for new levels.

We deal with the question, "Why?" We give not simply because the needs of the church are real, though they are. There are possibilities for strengthening, enabling development, enhancing growth of young and mature alike that are very exciting. But the basic issue is not "What is your share of the budget?" but "What is God's share of your income?" Not "What does the church need?" but "What does God want?"

Aute L. Carr suggests that "everything we possess in life is on loan. It could all be stamped 'on consignment.' Whatever we consume is gone; whatever we attempt to keep for ourselves will have to be given up in the end. The only thing we can really keep is what we give away. Reach out and touch someone in need and you widen the horizons of the soul, expand your spiritual vision and understanding, increase your capacity for sympathy and love.... Every time you give in Christ's name, your participation in the eternal life of the spirit and in the peace of God increases! You become more of a real person." (*Christian Ministry*, September 1979, p.36)

We also deal with the question, "What?" A tithe or 10 percent has been a plumb line since biblical days: sometimes the goal, sometimes the norm, sometimes the base on top of which additional gifts are possible. It is no magic formula. God does not expect us to go hungry and build mammoth church buildings, nor is God happy when we tithe while squandering the other 90 percent. The Gallup organization was commissioned by a coalition of 650 not-for-profit organizations, corporate foundations, and volunteer groups to research American giving patterns. What they discovered was surprising: moderately poor families are more generous than upper-middle-class families. Those with household incomes of $18,000 or less gave 2.8 percent—almost double the 1.5 percent of those earning between $50,000 and $75,000. This study led them to suggest a "Give Five" campaign: donate 5 percent of income and five hours a week to charitable causes. That is not a tithe, obviously, but for many it is a significant challenge. Each person and each family must try honestly and reverently to find and express God's will. How does God want us to use the resources entrusted to us—those resources that we have "on consignment"?

The third question dealt with is always the most difficult—the "How?" question. There is the easy way. It is how I came into stewardship. I can remember being given an allowance—a quarter. It was understood that a nickel of that was for the offering plate. In addition, something would be given over and above on birthdays—usually a penny for every year of life. Then I got a job with a weekly income. That was a crucial time. Would my childhood giving pattern prove to be only the result of parental guidance? Would I continue to give a dime or a quarter? Or would I give a percentage of income, which would grow as my ability grew? It is easy to begin early giving 10 percent or more and to stay with that. It is also easier when husband and wife have similar values. That is the easy way.

Another is the "don't wait until you win the lottery" way. Take your present giving as a base and then tithe the increases in income. Simply give 10 percent of the added ability. Yes, it would be great to suddenly tithe cold turkey, but many think that is impossible, so they never get started with significant Christian stewardship. Take your present giving as the base and begin tithing the increased income that results through the rest of your career.

Still another way is also the "jerk and press" method: increase your giving by 1 percent of income (okay, one-half percent of income) next year. That will require a resetting of priorities; it will be more feasible in some years than others; and it will test commitment. Moving from 2.8 to 3.8 percent, from 5 to 6 percent, from 8 to 9 percent can be a thrilling part of a growing Christian life. Having "been rooted and grounded in love," may you now understand the wider dimensions of the growing Christian life—the breadth, length, height, and depth. And may you experience the love of Christ that surpasses all we know or do.

III. For the Faithful

We also hear a message for the consistent, sacrificing, generous stewards of the years: Thank God (literally) for what you have made possible because of years of hard labor. Because of faithful stewardship through schooling, through depression and recession, through the education of children, through the transition to retirement; because of your thoughtfulness in writing your last will and testament so as to provide for the church after your death—you must be the ones mentioned in Ephesians: I pray "that you may be filled with all the fullness of God."

What does the phrase "the fullness of God" connote? For a Christian it could not be material gain, for our giving is unselfish in motive. It would rather be the knowledge that our giving, our stewardship, has not been in vain. There is a purpose in what we have done. We have been part of the strengthening of one church which has made impacts for good in a moderate-sized city with an educational center. We have cooperated with God in a mighty and valuable work. We trust God to use our efforts to affect human history.

Some may wonder if their offerings on each Sunday will help nations settle their differences. Who can say that they won't? Who can say that our gifts do not help an Indian woman to see, a South African youth to cling to hope, an Argentinean farmer to rotate crops better, or a Japanese mother to have a larger worldview? Who can deny that our gifts help Puerto Ricans both on the Caribbean island and on the island of Manhattan to maintain dignity?

Thank God for the missionaries, for the homes for needy persons, for church school classes where lives are molded, for the corner on which this church sits which reminds thousands of passers-by of their Creator whom they cannot pass by forever. These are ministries you have made possible through your consistent, faithful, dedicated stewardship.

A person is a Christian in that moment when he or she makes the first commitment, but it takes a lifetime to become a follower of Christ. You know how hard is the struggle and how impossible the goal, but may you—because of the knowledge that your labor will be continued and is important—"be filled with the fullness of God."

This chapter closes with a benediction: "Now to him who by the power at work within us is able to accomplish abundantly far more than all we can ask or imagine...." Remember when you didn't think you could afford to give so much? Could you have dreamed a few years ago that you would be taking the church so seriously? How can you move on from here? God enables us to do far more abundantly than all that we ask or think. "To him be glory in the church and in Christ Jesus to all generations, forever and ever. Amen."

Here ends the third chapter in the letter to the Ephesians. How shall the current chapter of our lives be concluded? It is the chapter in which we decide, in which we may grow, in which we can undergird.

BAREFOOT IN THE BAPTISTRY

Mary Donovan Turner

> *This is a fresh witness to hope and its power to move us to renewed commitment. It attaches the experience of anxiety and hope to the ritual of baptism. In our world where people are detached from the Christian tradition, we need to tie our preaching on management of life to concrete experiences of immersion in the church ritual and in the world.*

Isaiah 11:1–9

Last summer I went on a spiritual pilgrimage. No, not to Jerusalem or Bethlehem. Better. I went to Shreveport, Louisiana. With my mother and sister I traveled back to the place of my earliest childhood memories.

We arrived in the city late on a Friday evening and got up quite early on Saturday morning to look around the town and find the places where we had grown up—our schools, our stores, the homes of our friends, and our own home, which was now surprisingly small. But most of all we wanted to see the church. I had not been inside the sanctuary of that church since my family had moved from Louisiana some thirty years before. Early on Saturday morning we were able to enter. It was quiet—the quiet that a Saturday morning in a church usually affords.

I walked through the church kitchen and remembered how my mom and dad used to spend every Sunday night there preparing meals for the youth. I walked through the Sunday School classrooms and conjured up in my mind the faces of all the "saints" who had taught my classes. I had long forgotten many of their names, but they were saints nonetheless! And then

Mary Donovan Turner is associate professor of homiletics at Pacific School of Religion in Berkeley, California.

when I was alone, I walked into the stillness of the sanctuary and immersed myself in childhood memories. I saw the pew where the Donovan family always sat, the choir loft...and then my eye caught sight of the baptistry.

I was drawn to it; I couldn't stay away. So I went to the back hall behind the sanctuary and took off my tennis shoes and socks and quietly walked down the steps as if it were important that no one else know that I was there. I could feel the cool tiles against my bare feet, and memories began flooding back to me—what it was like that evening when as a ten-year-old I was baptized. I wanted to remember what must have been swirling around in the mind of a child who finds herself standing there by a large adult, a minister robed in white, all ready to immerse her into the pool of water. What did I hope for? What did I feel? Was I excited or nervous? Calm or peaceful? As I stood there at the age of 41, barefoot in the baptistry, I could remember one thing for sure. I knew that as a ten-year-old I understood that I was doing something very important. I knew that because I was being immersed in that water my life would be changed. I remember thinking as a ten-year-old that I wanted to give everything I could—*give everything I could*—to the God who had called me there. A person could not make a life commitment more seriously than I did that evening so long ago. I would not, of course, as a ten-year-old, ever have used the word, but I knew that I was making a covenant.

Standing there in that baptistry remembering the mystery and wonder of that night, I was swept by a strange sadness. I couldn't quite identify it at first, that overwhelming sense of sadness. But as I stood there looking out over that grand sanctuary with light pouring through the stained glass windows, I knew. I knew that the covenant I had made to give all that I had was sincerely made...and not always kept. Into the magic of the moment had crept the realities of life as I had lived it, and a sadness swept over me. I hadn't known on that evening when I was ten that the promises I made, the commitments that I had intended to keep, were not as easy as I had at first imagined. I couldn't have known that life would be filled with such complexity, that even when I wanted to live up to my commitment of "gift giving to God," I would sometimes not know how, or even whether I had. I just didn't know how difficult it would be to be a covenantal partner—a partner whose eyes could see beyond the sanctuary walls that even now in the quietness of the Saturday morning separated me from the world. I knew as I stood there barefoot in the baptistry that my vision had been too narrow, my world too small. And I also knew that I was not alone. It has always been difficult to be a covenantal partner with God.

"Can't you see?" Isaiah said to the people gathered around him. "Can't you see that you no longer even know God? Do you see that child—that orphan? Gnawing hunger has made his bones protrude. God is disappointed," Isaiah said, "in the sacrifices you toss casually upon the altar. You think you are giving what God desires, but God wants more. God wants you to learn about goodness, to seek justice, to rescue the oppressed. You have not understood. There is darkness. There is no light."

The people did not know when they made their commitments that life would be filled with such complexity. They didn't know that even when they wanted to live up to their covenantal obligations, even when they wanted to, they would not always be certain that they had. They often didn't know when they were calling good evil, and evil good. They didn't know that their values were confused and their vision blurry. They were self-satisfied, bringing sacrifices and tossing them to God. In God's eyes, Isaiah told them, they had become useless and decayed like the short jagged remains of a tree that has been toppled. Like a stump.

The editor of the book of Isaiah describes for us in verse after verse this "covenant gone astray" people. We feel the hopelessness and the utter desperateness of their plight. We have lived there.

Then suddenly and without warning the editor inserts a shocking word, an unexpected word of hope. "Stop! Wait! This won't always be. A shoot will grow out of the stump. A branch will grow out of the roots. Wait! Wait! Our life together won't always be this way! The wolf will live with the lamb, and the leopard will live with the kid—natural enemies will live in peace. Wait! Some day there will be a world with no violence. The children will be safe—those for whom nightmares are a daily reality—they will be safe, all of them. Someday even the weakest and most vulnerable among us will not have to fear."

The editor of the book of Isaiah knew that we must come face to face with the realities of the world in which we live and how we have chosen to live there. But sometimes we must stop and rise above all that swirls around us and "catch hold of the vision" not of what is, but what *can be*.

That's what I came to know as I stood there barefooted on that baptistry tile on a Saturday morning in Shreveport, Louisiana. I had spent much of my life inside the sanctuary walls, where life was safe and quiet and protected. I had shut out the cries of the people in the world around me. No longer did I see the man huddled in his worn blanket sitting on the streets looking for only a morsel. I didn't commit violence, but neither did I work creatively to stop it. I was not giving all I could to the God who had called me—at least I was not giving what God would want of me. But wait. Stop! What would the world be like if I did seek justice...rescue the oppressed. If we did?

I reclaimed that morning the gnawing desire to be a covenant person. I was now a little wiser than I was at ten. I knew that perhaps it wouldn't be easy. The journey would never be over. But I climbed those steps out of the baptistry and I sat down and I put on my tennis shoes and socks, and I smiled.

For a moment, a very brief moment, I was able to rise above the realities of life around me and in me. I had once again "caught hold of the vision."

WATERS OF ONENESS

Dan P. Moseley

> *This sermon struggles where people struggle—in a divided and fragmented world. It reveals the connection between the practice of baptism and the sense of wholeness in one's self. Salvation is experienced when the whole self is baptized into the whole community. This points to the church's responsibility to deal with the whole person and the whole world and to be good stewards of body, mind, heart, and soul.*

Genesis 1:1–5, Mark 1:4–11

I

A mother came to me recently and said, "I don't know what I am going to do. It is utter chaos in my life. I move from soccer to band practice to church. I move then to the grocery store, to my job. My children have activities that they need to go to. I have to take them to the doctor. It seems like I never, never stop. I never slow down."

A man confessed to me recently. "You may think I've got it together, but underneath this facade it feels like the world is falling apart. I don't know if I can hold it together much longer. My job is demanding and changing. I may lose my job. My children depend on me. My wife depends on me. Others in the community depend on me. I try to be a faithful participant in this community. I am active in the Lions Club. I try to be involved in the church, but there is too much going on. My life is spinning out of control."

A teenager confessed to me. "I am scared. I am confused. I don't know what I want to do. My parents think I ought to go to college, but I think I want to work. Some people think I ought to get married when I get older, but I don't want to get

Dan Moseley is the Herald D. Monroe Professor of Practical Ministry at Christian Theological Seminary, Indianapolis, Indiana, and is the editor of this collection of sermons.

married. I am afraid of what people are going to think of me. I don't know what to do with my life. My parents are on me all the time. I am confused and distracted all the time, and I can't study."

No matter who we are or in what stage of life we find ourselves, most of us experience at some time or another such fragmentation and disorientation as this. Our lives are moving in so many directions that there seems never to be any place that we can rest. There seems never to be any center for our lives on which we can stand that does not move or shift every minute of every day.

The culture we live in doesn't help us. The culture we live in contributes to the same disorientation because there are so many demands, so much going on, and so much confusion all around us.

Last Wednesday evening, on my way from home to church, I decided I was going to see how much distraction there really was. So I counted the number of signs there are between the church and my house. It takes about ten minutes to drive. Do you know how many signs there are between my house, seven miles away, and here? The Vine Street Christian Church sign right in front is number 413.

Distractions! We get to where we don't even notice them, but they are there calling out, reminding us, calling us to buy and to sell. Reminding us where to go and how fast to go. Always distractions.

It used to be that you opened the newspaper and it was generic news. Now, there is the national news, the environmental news, and the health news. This is all in the first section of news. Then there is the local news and then there is the sports section. Right? No. There are two sports sections. There is the football sports section and then there is the rest of the sports. Then there are the living, business, RSVP, and food sections.

Life is fragmented. It is just all over the place. It all falls out when you are drinking your coffee in the morning.

Doctors. Did you ever have a family doctor? I did, once. Now there are pediatricians, foot doctors, nose doctors, ear doctors, bowel doctors, and bladder doctors. There is a doctor for every part of the body. Who ever deals with the whole self? Where is it that one becomes united and centered?

II

Our world doesn't help us a lot. And yet, in spite of the world we live in, there is deep within us a yearning, a desire to see things bound together, to hold them together, to be focused, to have our lives focused with energy around one thing instead of being distracted by so many things that seem sometimes to matter and other times not to amount to a hill of beans.

Now, occasionally, we are focused. Occasionally, we have clarity of purpose. Occasionally, it comes to us, and usually it is a crisis. Usually it is when someone gets sick. When someone gets sick, there is no question about what matters most. When someone has a baby, nothing else really matters, does it? It does not matter; everything focuses on one thing.

But who wants to wait for a crisis to order our lives? Who wants a crisis to be the thing that centers your life, to give you some sense of purpose and value in your life? Religion is supposed to do it. That's the purpose of religion. The word *religion* means "to rebind; to bind together again; to bind you with that which gives you your sense of wholeness and purpose." It is to pull you together and make you whole. That's the purpose of religion.

Now, admittedly religion has often been inadequate in representing that kind of wholeness, that kind of salvation. Admittedly, when you come to church you may feel as fragmented as you did before you got here. You come here. We put the children in one place, the young people in another, and the adults in another place. We divide people up into age groups. Fragmented.

But the purpose of religion is to center yourself. It is to be that agent that gives you a sense of purpose and wholeness, a sense of oneness. When you are truly faithful to that which you believe, you have a sense of what it is you are about.

III

Now, Jesus—as simple as this seems to those of us who are sophisticated and educated and have all kinds of doubts—is the central person in our religious tradition. He is the model of what it means to be centered, to be whole, to be at one with God. He is that model; and if we look at him, we begin to understand the way in which we might find that wholeness, that salvation. That's what the word *salvation* means in the Bible. It means wholeness, "at one with God."

In the text that was read this morning, we read about Jesus and his baptism. Jesus went into the waters of baptism, into the Jordan, and was baptized by John. Now, some may wonder why Jesus did that. It says that people came confessing their sins and were baptized. Some of us have been taught that Jesus did not sin, that Jesus was sinless and pure. Why is it that Jesus, then, chose to be baptized?

If you read the book of Mark and you read that section in its context, you get a clue. Mark says they came from all of Jerusalem, from all of Judea; all the people came to be baptized by John in the Jordan.

Is this the reason Jesus came? Because he belongs to "all the people"? Is the witness of Jesus' baptism that he is a part of all people and he is not separate, but he is one with all? Is that a clue that what it means to be at one, at peace with God, is to recognize that you are a part of all the people?

You know how difficult and disorienting it is when in your family there is tension or conflict, when you are not at one. You know how much energy it takes just to try to keep a semblance of order when you are not one with each other. You have been in churches in your lifetime when people were not one with each other. They were at odds, bickering and complaining all the time. How much energy was dissipated away from the mission of the church by those who could not agree on how to be one? It is hard to keep yourself centered if you are not at one with all the people.

So Jesus in his baptism chose to be one with the people. If we are to be centered in our religious life, we too must be one with the community of faith and with the tradition, the family stories of our faith. We must know those stories and be a part of those stories. When we are, we understand what happens when we are baptized into the faith. We are baptized, the scriptures say, into the body of Christ. To be baptized into the body of Christ is to be baptized into his grace and into responsibility. When you are baptized into the body of Christ, you are baptized into the one who is merciful, the one who represents God's eternal gift of love and life for you. When you are baptized into the body of Christ, you are embraced by the waters of baptism. In the arms of the representative of God, you are embraced by the waters of baptism and reminded that your life is a gift. It is not your own, but you live by the very breath of God.

When you are baptized, you are reminded how precious life is, and you celebrate the love that God washes over you. When you are baptized, you are baptized a whole person. When you go into the waters of baptism, and you go under the waters, no part of you is left out; you are wholly baptized. Why? Because your whole life is under God's grace—your body, your mind, your heart, your soul, your whole life. Not just the part that you want, and think is good. Your anger, your sadness, your grief, your illness, your strength, your power, your creativity—everything, everything is immersed in the grace of God.

IV

That's what it means to be baptized into the body of Christ. It is to be baptized into the mercy and compassion of God. Jesus came and was baptized with all the folks and became one with humanity in the arms of God, representing God's grace and love.

But that's not all. When you are baptized, you are wholly baptized into the body of Christ, and not only are you embraced by grace, you are given some sense of obligation and responsibility to serve that body of Christ. We do not live as whole human beings if all we do is receive and take into ourselves. To be whole, to be healthy, to be saved, is to be one who not only is embraced by grace, but also takes the obligation and responsibility for the grace-filled community.

There are those who do not think that is what they need to do. There are those who believe that all you can do is receive, and it is okay. But we have seen in our own lifetimes what happens when human beings simply take. The planet on which we live is crying out because we have failed to put back into it all that we have been taking out. Sure, we can take the coal from the mountain. We can take the trees from the hills. We can take the water, fill it with pollution. We can do all those things, but one day, friends, it will not give life back unless we give it ourselves now. We cannot keep taking.

How many of you have tried with your bank to keep taking without ever putting anything back? They will let you know soon rather than late.

This body of Christ has filled this community and has filled us with grace, but it cannot keep giving unless we who have received give back. Not simply of our minds, not simply of our presence, but of our whole selves. Our whole selves were baptized into the body.

You see, if you want to be religious part-time, if you just want to love God with your mind, you will find God to be just another fragmenting factor in your life. There will be no centering power if you want to commit yourself only part-time. It is those who commit themselves in baptism wholly—who commit their minds, their hearts, their bodies, their souls, to devotion to God—who then begin to get a glimpse of salvation, of wholeness, of health, and have their lives centered.

Fragmentation will prevail if we do not get some sense of focus. Disorientation will be the result of our lack of discipline about our own spiritual life. We will be distracted and divided in ourselves until the time when we can wholly give ourselves to the divine. When that occurs, we will experience and celebrate salvation with God.

$\mathcal{M}$ANDATE FOR GIVING

R. Robert Cueni

What is the relationship between death and money?
Both create fear. Therefore, each is a matter of faith.
This sermon explores "in a unique way" the issue of
resurrection and giving. It puts both death and money in
their proper place. This is a creative, fresh way to
approach commitment Sunday.

1 Corinthians 15:52—16:2

As we move to this latter part of the fifteenth chapter of 1 Corinthians, we can feel the momentum starting to build. For paragraph after paragraph, Paul has been thinking through the implications of something he said about the resurrection of Jesus Christ. If you open your imagination as you read, you can almost see the wheels grinding in this man's great mind as he moves from implication to conclusion, to new implication, to yet another conclusion. He begins, "Let me remind you of Jesus the Christ, who was crucified, buried and raised to life on the third day."

Then it occurs to Paul that the resurrection of our Lord has implications for us. "And if Jesus was raised from the dead, then we can believe that God can raise us from the dead."

Paul goes on to wrestle with some of the questions posed by saying that we too shall be raised. For instance, "Some people are going to wonder about the resurrection body. Well," to paraphrase Paul thinking aloud, "a resurrected body will probably be different. The present body will have the same relationship to the resurrected body as an apple seed has to the apple tree that grows from it. It will be entirely different, yet somehow obviously related."

Robert Cueni is senior minister of Country Club Christian Church in Kansas City, Missouri, and the author of *What Ministers Can't Learn in Seminary.*

At that point we can almost see the light bulb flash on over Paul's head. In a moment of insight it occurs to him, "Oh, wow! Do you realize what that means? We are talking about the fact that because of what God has done in Christ Jesus, we don't have to face the greatest enemy of the human species. God has conquered death. Its power is broken. Death cannot destroy us. We have nothing to fear."

Paul is now racing down the runway getting up speed to fly. "Listen to this secret; we shall not all die, but in an instant we shall all be changed, as quickly as the blinking of an eye, when the last trumpet sounds. For when it sounds, the dead will be raised and we shall all be changed." And when that happens, "then the scripture will come true: 'death is destroyed; victory is complete!' Where, Death, is your victory? Where, Death, is your power to hurt?" (1 Corinthians 16:54–55, TEV).

Paul is now at the pinnacle of inspirational soaring. He is flying high, but he doesn't leave us to enjoy this panoramic view. From these lofty inspirational heights Paul moves instantly to talk about implications. He concludes this fifteenth chapter by reminding his readers that since we don't have to worry about anything, including death, we should live courageously and righteously. William Barclay paraphrases Paul's thinking in this last couple of verses of 1 Corinthians 15 by saying that we should live faithful Christian lives no matter what because the rewards are so great. We can face anything because not even death is our enemy. Since we are inevitable winners, we can live like winners.

When those Christians in Corinth got this letter, I bet they were out of breath when they came to verse 58. Their friend Paul had taken them to the mountain top. They had seen the Promised Land. "Death, where is your victory? Death, where is your power to hurt?" Whatever we do in the service of God is to be valued. Amen and amen. With a bit of imagination, as you come to the end of 1 Corinthians 15 you can hear the choir of angels and archangels singing with the Kansas City Symphony in the background. This is inspirational stuff.

That is what makes the opening of the sixteenth chapter so startling. From "Death, where is your victory?" Paul continues, "Now the matter about the money to be raised to help God's people in Judea...." This is one of the most abrupt transitions in the entire scripture. In fact, some scholars have suggested that some later editor must have cut and pasted these verses together because Paul would not have abandoned the spiritual discussion so abruptly in favor of talking about the offering.

Paul does go from the mountaintop of inspiration to the valley of the practical. We might expect Jerry Falwell or Oral Roberts to do something like this, but not Paul. It is almost as if he is saying, "Enough of the sermon; let's get on with the offering. I've ceased preaching; now get out your wallets and your checkbooks because we have to keep the overhead paid. Consider our offering for the month. For fifty shillings a month you can become a member of the Corinthian Club; 250 shillings a month puts you in the Kingdom of God Club and you get a King James Version of the Bible with National Geographic maps and words of Jesus marked in red."

Of course, I am exaggerating. Actually these two chapters of 1 Corinthians are not as disjointed as they first appear. Paul does go directly from the resurrection to the offering, but that doesn't mean he goes from the wonderful world of spiritual matters to the dark world of the practical. These are both spiritual issues, and he stays right on the topic of how we can live lives of faithful Christians because we are God's children and we don't have anything to fear.

Remember, the missionary journeys of Paul had three purposes: 1) preaching the good news of the risen Savior to all who would listen; 2) helping organize new churches; and 3) the very practical assignment of raising money for the poor Christians in Jerusalem.

Times had been tough for the Christian community in the capital city; Jewish-Roman relationships had been strained for years, and they were now moving toward open revolt. In fact, within the next decade or so from the writing of 1 Corinthians, the Romans were to crush a Jewish uprising, deport many Jews, and nearly destroy Jerusalem—actually leveling most public buildings, including the temple.

Because both the Jews and the Romans discriminated against them, Christians were among the poorest people in the city. As the political situation worsened, circumstances got worse and worse for the apostles and other followers of Jesus who remained in Jerusalem. They were pushed further and further to the social, political, and economic fringes of the city. As resources for all people became limited with the approach of open revolution, Christians suffered more than others. The Romans were tough on the Jews, but circumstances made the Christians suffer even more. The old non-biblical proverb held then as now: "When it rains on the rich, they get wet; when it rains on the poor they drown."

It was for this reason that Paul was assigned the task of collecting an offering from the other Christian churches to help care for the needs of the "saints in Jerusalem." In his journeys, Paul collected money in Phillipi from the Phillipians, in Thessalonica from the Thessalonians, in Ephesus from the Ephesians, and from all those other New Testament places.

This offering was not considered something other than a matter of faith. It was definitely a spiritual issue. In fact, the topic of being generous with our money follows logically from a discussion of death. Probably no two topics are closer to our hearts than our money and our physical lives. Just as we have a natural and terrible fear of parting with our lives, so we have a natural and terrible fear of parting with our money.

The response of faith is the same on both topics. Because of what God has done in Jesus Christ we don't have to be afraid of losing our lives or our fortunes. Our existence, our wholeness, our salvation is not dependent upon either money or a physical body. That is why it is a simple transition from Chapter 15 and the resurrection to Chapter 16 and the offering for the Christians in Jerusalem. The central truth is the same: We don't have to worry about dying because death cannot separate us from the love of God, and we don't have to worry about being generous with our money because even if we lost everything, poverty would not separate us from the love of God. We are to live as faithful, courageous Christians in the assurance that God will sustain us.

Now, of course, a theology of giving differs significantly from a theology of dying. Our two greatest fears may be the loss of life and the loss of money, but that is where the similarity ends. We do not face death and face the morning offering in the same way, with the same tools, or for the same reason.

This morning we celebrate Commitment Sunday. It is a time we ask you as the people of this congregation to make a commitment of your blessings for the work of Christ's church. Even though that commitment is between you and God, we ask you to inform the treasurer of the church what your giving plans are for the next fiscal year so the church can build its spending plan. We all have a chance to do that later in this service of worship. First of all, however, I want to mention a couple of things for your prayerful consideration:

1. If you want your money to be as much a spiritual issue as Paul tells us it should be, don't permit your material possessions to assume a place of importance in your life greater

than they deserve. Actually, money is no big deal. I know you think it is mighty important. All of us do. That is part of our human condition, but money doesn't deserve the status we frequently give it. Keep this in mind: Your checkbook cannot save you. Even if you lost everything you had, God would still watch over you. There is no salvation by the wallet. But you already know that. Of this I am certain: The biggest difference between the rich and the poor is that the poor still think that if they had enough money, they could solve all their problems and live happily ever after. You know that doesn't happen. So treat your money for what it is—just another blessing God has given you.

2. I want to challenge you. Whatever you are giving right now to the life of the church, I challenge you to grow. Some of you may need to grow considerably; others may not be able to do that. But all of us can grow in our giving. I challenge you to plan to grow—not for the sake of the budget of the church, but for the sake of your own spiritual life.

I know that for some of you, that can be scary. But why not give it a chance and see what a wonderful sense of blessedness comes by growing as a steward?

Here again, Paul's words from 1 Corinthians 16:1–2: "Now the matter about the money to be raised to help God's people in Judea; you must do what I told the churches in Galatia to do. On the first day of every week each of you must put aside some money, in proportion to what you have earned, and save it up so there will be no need to collect money when I come" (paraphrase).

At the close of our service, we are going to have an opportunity to make our commitment to God and to the life of this church. Let us prayerfully prepare for that.

WHERE IS YOUR HEART?

Richard L. Hamm

> *Which comes first, the chicken or the egg? Commitment
> or contribution? According to this sermon, and Jesus,
> contributions come before commitment. Giving is
> followed by devotion. Stewardship is responding
> to grace and the result is a deepening spiritual life.*

Matthew 6:19–21

Most of us have heard this passage so many times that
we no longer hear it at all. We figure we understand it, and
there is nothing else in it for us. It is a straightforward, simple
proposition. But think about this passage again for a moment.
Jesus had a way of taking the obvious truths that everyone
accepts as common sense, the obvious truths that "go without
saying," and putting them in a new light.

What we *think* this passage says is, "Wherever your
heart is, there will your treasure be." That's what we hear
because that's the truth that "goes without saying." We all
know it is true that wherever our heart is, that's where our
treasure will be.

For example, if your heart is thrilled by cars, you will probably invest a good bit of your money in a car that your heart
really desires. If you love boats, you'll probably work hard to
obtain one that pleases you.

My wife long ago gave me one of those wall hangings that
says, "The only difference between men and boys is the price
of their toys." She gave me that right after I bought an
airplane...which I sold when our kids came along...which was

Richard Hamm is general minister and president of the Christian Church (Disciples
of Christ).

OK because our kids thrill my heart even more than did my airplane...which is saying a lot...but which basically means that, indeed, where our heart is, our money soon follows!

But Jesus doesn't *say*, "Where your heart is, there will your treasure be." *He* knows that's true; *we* know that's true; *everybody* knows that's true. It's obvious. What he does say is *also* true but more subtle...as matters of the spirit often are.

He says, "Where your treasure is, there your heart will be." Do you hear the difference? *Of course* we're going to invest where our heart is, but Jesus' point is that our heart will be where we invest! So the question this morning is, "Where is your heart?" Which is really the same question as, "Where do you invest your treasure?"

A couple of years ago, I invested a considerable amount of treasure in a new car. Now, it might not be what *you* would want in a car, but for me, it is perfect: fifteen-inch cast aluminum wheels, V-6, touring suspension, in "black cherry"!

It is *my baby*! When my son went to get his driver's license and took his road test in it, I just about fainted. In those first months of ownership, I alienated my wife and children because I insisted on parking the thing a half mile from the doors of the mall where no one else parks so there was no chance of people dinging it when they opened their doors! My family was *praying* someone would ding it, so this would be over with and I'd start treating it like a car. That was probably the most serious idolatry going on in my life right then! But it passed.

These things to which we attach ourselves do become burdens. You know the old saying: "The two happiest days in a man's life are the day he buys his boat...and the day he sells his boat."

Wherever we invest our treasure, that's where our hearts will be. Wherever we invest our time, our talent, our energy, and our money, that's where our hearts will be.

When Jesus says, "Where your treasure is, there your heart will be," he is making a plea. He is saying, "If you want to be closer to God, then invest in the kingdom of God, and your heart will follow." You see, this is a *spiritual* issue! Your life will be driven and directed and dominated by whatever it is you invest your treasure in. What do you want to have on the throne of your life? *Things*? Or *God*? If we want God on the throne of our lives, then we need to invest in the kingdom of God, and our hearts will soon follow.

Recently, a pastor (who shall go unnamed) bragged to me that he hadn't preached a stewardship sermon in some sixteen years. He's proud of that! But let me tell you about his congregation. They pay this part-time pastor with money they receive from people who rent their parsonage. They give nothing to mission within or beyond their own town, and they are in deep conflict. Is it any wonder? Their treasure is going elsewhere, so their hearts are elsewhere, too. The pastor should be ashamed. Instead of leading that congregation into the kingdom, he's letting it go to hell! And he's proud of it!

Lots of preachers, it seems, find it difficult to talk about stewardship. Why is that? My hunch is they fear talking about stewardship because they don't really understand what it is themselves. They think stewardship means "paying the church's bills," including their salaries, and so they feel self-conscious about it.

What most congregations call a stewardship campaign is not really a stewardship campaign. It's really a campaign to raise the budget. The argument for giving usually boils down to something like this: "We have this many members and this big a budget, so your fair share is this much." Oh boy! That's exciting! I don't get to pay bills at home, so I really cherish the opportunity to pay the church's bills. What a spiritual blessing!

So what exactly *is* Christian stewardship?

In the broadest sense, Christian stewardship means taking care of God's world: the environment, the people, the flora and the fauna. It means taking care of the resources God has provided us—the time, the talent, the money—using these resources in ways that are pleasing in God's sight.

You don't believe these things are God-given? We brought none of it into the world with us, and we'll take none of it out of the world with us. When J. D. Rockefeller died, there was much speculation about his net worth. A reporter asked Rockefeller's attorney, "How much did he leave?" The attorney replied, "All of it!"

You never saw a funeral procession with a Brinks truck nor even so much as a U-Haul trailer!

It all belongs to God, but it's on loan to us for a time.

Stewardship means taking care of God's world, taking care of the resources God has given us, *and* this morning we need to recognize that it means responding to God's love by giving gifts for the work of the kingdom. To put it another way, as Christians we are called to give out of *gratitude* for all that God has given to us.

I think it was easier to be grateful to God for the simple things of life like food and shelter when people lived closer to raw nature. We who live in the cities and towns of America forget that food isn't really manufactured. It is grown—grown through the efforts of men and women who nurture the soil and the seed against the sometimes cruel forces of weather. Every kernel of corn we consume, every grain of wheat or rice, every piece of fruit represents a miracle of God's ongoing creation and providence for our sakes. We need to look past our insulation and recognize anew that all good things come from God.

Paul once wrote, "Give thanks in all circumstances." That is pretty far removed from where most of us live, but it is good advice. We would do well to develop our sense of dependence upon God and to develop our sense of gratitude for all God's gifts.

How do we develop grateful hearts? How do we give our hearts more completely to God? We invest—in the kingdom.

Where is your heart? Today is a significant opportunity to invest, that your heart may follow. I'm not asking you to give your fair share of the budget. I'm asking you to respond to God's love and grace in your life. I'm asking you to *invest* where you want your heart to be...because it *will* follow.

*L*OOKING FOR *T*REASURE IN *A*LL THE *R*IGHT *P*LACES

Diane Elston Clark

> *Sometimes ministers are excessive in prescribing solutions. This excess often makes the prescription useless to the person receiving it. This sermon does not err in that way. It creates many questions and, thus, stimulates the thinking of the hearer. In this sense, it does what Jesus did with many of his parables. This sermon is recommended as a way of inviting the hearers to finish the sermon in their own lives in the real world.*

Matthew 13:44–52

Do you know the message of John the Baptist as he came preaching to the people? And when Jesus began to preach, even after John was arrested and killed, what did Jesus say? Their message was the same: "Repent, for the kingdom of heaven is at hand."

Strange words, aren't they, for people who consider themselves God's elect? But they are words that reverberate through the ages, calling to us yet, catching us up short, making us look at ourselves and our lives anew to see if we are acting like God's elect—to see if we truly belong to the kingdom of heaven, to see if we know anything about what Jesus calls the treasure that satisfies.

Each week we bow our heads and pray, "Thy kingdom come, thy will be done, on *earth* as it is in heaven." And Jesus teaches over and over again about the kingdom of heaven. "The kingdom of heaven is like treasure hidden in a field, which someone found and hid; then in his joy he goes and sells all that he has and buys that field." (Matthew 13:44.) Or: "The kingdom of heaven is like a merchant in search of fine pearls; on finding one pearl of great value, he went and sold all that he had and bought it." (13:45.)

Diane Clark is pastor of First Christian Church in Llano, Texas.

And: "The kingdom of heaven is like a net that was thrown into the sea and caught fish of every kind...." (Matthew 13:47.) "The kingdom of heaven is like a mustard seed....like yeast that a woman took and mixed in with three measures of flour until all of it was leavened." (13:31, 33.) It is like "someone who sowed good seed in his field" (13:24).

Did you ever notice that Jesus never defines the kingdom of heaven? He only speaks in parables, giving us little pictures— giving us many questions. Do you wonder why he does that? He focuses often and in varied ways on the kingdom, as if people just don't get it. Do they get it but find it hard to accept? Or do most people fail to get it? Do *we* get it?

After all, we are kingdom people, are we not? We *think* we are kingdom people. But just when we think we are kingdom people, Jesus catches us up short, and we realize that maybe we don't know so much about the kingdom after all.

We spend so much of our time in our own little kingdoms— this world, our job, our community, our home, our school, our family, our friends. We build our tabernacles of our own personal concerns—the storehouses of our treasures on earth. We build our kingdom on sand, which shifts and sinks and washes away, and our faith is shaken.

We see ourselves as the chosen people and close our eyes to our own sins. We believe in Christ. We attend church regularly. We share some of what we have with others. We live the best we can. What *more* could God want?

Maybe God would want us to wipe the scales from our eyes that we might see ourselves more clearly. Maybe God would want us to see that there is *nothing* on which we can depend in this world. Maybe God would want us to leave behind our infatuation with worldly wealth. Maybe God would want us to be able to lay all that we have and all that we are on God's altar and say, "Here I am. Here is everything I have. I give it all and I give myself to you."

Jesus came teaching that the kingdom of God is at hand. We ask, "What does that mean?" We fail to understand. Again, he doesn't give definitions. He offers parables and leaves much to our imaginations. We look so hard for the kingdom of God, and Jesus says it's "at hand." It's "nearby." So maybe, just maybe, the kingdom is right before our eyes in big and little things that we take for granted. Could that be? Could it be right here among us?

Could it be that the kingdom of heaven is here when we help another person, when we sit with the ill, when we comfort the grieving, when we give a scholarship to a college student, when we put food in the town pantry, when we make baby layettes or school kits, when we decide to give our best to God—perhaps even to tithe, or more?

Could it be that the kingdom of heaven is to be found in our concern for one another or in our acceptance of those who are different from us? Could it be that the kingdom of heaven is with us when we welcome strangers, when we patch up a quarrel, when we give our gifts at the altar, when we ask forgiveness, when *we* forgive?

Could the kingdom of heaven be in the outpouring of gifts, of food and drink, of meat and cookies, of cleaning supplies, of money, in the caring, in the generosity of time given, in the muscle and sweat of filling sandbags or cleaning up after a flood?

Could it be that the kingdom of heaven is *absent* when we do not do these things, when we are too self-absorbed, when all we care about is our own lives, our jobs, our families, or how we get ahead? Is that why Jesus first tells us to *repent* before he announces that God's kingdom is at hand? Could it be that if we repent we will see the kingdom? If we repent we will know the kingdom is at hand, in our midst?

Could it be that if we turn again to God, with our whole hearts and minds and souls, the scales will fall from our eyes and we will find that holy treasure? Will we see the great outpouring of God's love and grace and know it is for us and for all humanity?

We have to know, when we witness an outpouring of gifts such as we saw for the flood victims, that God's kingdom surely is at hand, surely is among us. And we have to know it is a treasure that truly satisfies, like nothing else at all. Could it be that God is working with us always, in big or small things, whether we see it or not?

The kingdom of heaven is like a wise person who built a house on solid rock. The winds came and the rains fell, but the house did not fall because it was built on rock (Matthew 7:24–25). Jesus is the rock who can keep us from falling, no matter what the storm. Jesus is the rock who can lead us to the kingdom of heaven where God reigns forever.

And when we find it, we know it is the greatest treasure, a treasure not to be hoarded but to be given away! For we find that the more we give it away, the more it is ours. The more we share our Christ, the more he is with us. The more we give, of ourselves or our goods, the greater is our joy and satisfaction.

Could it be that it is in giving and doing and serving and helping others that we find God's greatest treasures? For those treasures are joy and love and peace. How can we have those if we do not know how to give or to share?

There was a woman who had lost her husband and her child. Her heart grew cold. She wept and mourned. One day she went to find solace from her priest, who told her she could find peace if she found five homes that had only been blessed and had never known pain. So she began to knock on doors. At every house she found there had been pain. But she listened, and she learned to console. She gave of herself and her money to ease pains and woes. Her heart became so touched by others' woes that she enlisted others to go and help too.

She learned a great secret. It was in giving herself that she found God's kingdom, and that was a treasure that truly satisfied.

$\mathcal{G}$OD OR GOVERNMENT?

John Wade Payne

Sometimes answers are best left unsaid, especially if they are unknown. This sermon is a good illustration of the strengths of an understanding of stewardship by the citizens of two realms—the kingdom of God and the kingdoms of the earth. The struggle honestly shared and clarified may hold its own answers. Try it.

Matthew 22:15–22

"Give to the emperor what is the emperor's and give to God what is God's." Clever fellow, Jesus. He confounded his questioners who were trying to get him publicly to betray his own cause. They used flattery in an attempt to get Jesus to drop his guard: "Teacher, you're true blue, and don't care about rank or position." Then they virtually dared him to be reckless and revolutionary. In effect they said, "Hey, Jesus, come on, stop worrying; tell us, your friends and admirers, what you really think about those Romans who occupy our land and rip us off with their corrupt taxation."

Whichever way Jesus answered, he was trapped. If he answered "God," treason against Rome. If he answered the "emperor," blasphemy against God. Jesus' coin trick was brilliant as a way to avoid choosing either option. It was also a brilliant answer for the early Christians who struggled to find their dual roles as subjects of the imperial governor and as members of a sometimes bitterly persecuted community, the church. It was a brilliant answer for much of history, when people were ruled by both divine-right kings and divine-right church.

But what about us? "Give to the emperor what is the emperor's, and give to God what is God's." It echoes in the mind

John Wade Payne is senior pastor of Park Avenue Christian Church in New York, New York.

with another oft-quoted phrase that has been at least as controversial: "separation of church and state."

When the government is a foreign power, aligned with another religious tradition, Jesus' answer to a few unusually wily Pharisees is on target. But who is Caesar in a government which at least gives lip service to be—and at its best really is—of and for and by the people? Can we separate the exclusive business of church from the exclusive business of state? It challenges us with the gamut of questions from required prayers in school to whether one can be excused from required military service because of conscientious objection to war.

It's obvious that Americans, including American Christians, have not done very well at sorting out between church and state, between sacred and secular—between what is the emperor's and what is God's. Examples abound—some deeply troubling, some absurd, some both—such as the clash in the courts, Congress, and state legislatures over women's right to have a role in their reproductive destiny, in a climate where certain religious commitments abhor and reject both contraception and abortion. Hillary Rodham Clinton wore a small cross on a necklace at one of the presidential inauguration events, and some media commentators couldn't wait to comment on how inappropriate this was on a state occasion. The cry for government monies for church-sponsored schools is alive and well across the nation, especially among people who preach the loudest about getting the government out of their lives.

The problem in sorting out what is the emperor's and what is God's is that we can't. Yet we love to sort things out, to organize our lives into compartments. Our newspapers and news programs are full of graphs, polls—what percentage of us is this, that, or the other? Is there a world of business and another of religion? Can one park her or his Christian commitment just outside the curtain of the voting booth? Through the decades plenty have tried. By reducing the Christian faith to a moralistic preparation for a future next-world "sweet-by-and-by," all kinds of current this-world injustices—from slavery, slum landlords, and poverty-producing wages, to life-threatening work conditions—could be ignored by Bible-toting, self-righteous people absolutely certain that they were both good Americans and good Christians. They went to church on Sunday, prayed over every meal—and were exactly like those few wily Pharisees who tried to trick Jesus into betraying his mission. Some of this absurdity thankfully is history; but too much of it remains alive and well among us.

What in life can be separated from the realm of God? Where would you draw the line? Are some taxes that we pay part of God's work and some not? I can make a strong case that the portion of my taxes that goes to Medicaid, WIC programs, refugee hospitality, hospital construction, education, Head Start, public housing, National Endowment for the Arts, job training, unemployment insurance, and much of fire and police protection are all part of what God intends us to do on earth. They can be called God's work. At one time the church took care of nearly every one of those programs. Hospitals, schools, and almost all programs for the poor in western society were all run by the churches.

But what about the taxes I paid when our government was fighting a deeply controversial war in Vietnam, or in the Persian Gulf? What about all those nuclear devices you and I helped fund that could destroy human life a hundred times over, that now the government must pay more millions to deactivate? What about all those people who made magnificent sums on now defunct savings and loan institutions that you and I must salvage with our taxes? And what about the funds our government contributes to the World Bank, ostensibly to help poor nations, but which too often leave the poor impoverished while enriching banks here?

I doubt that you came to church to hear lists like these this morning. But that question put to Jesus won't leave us alone. How do we make decisions about Caesar and God, church and state, things spiritual and things temporal in a society which is rightly involved in all of life, and worship a God faith claims is rightly involved in all of life?

The many questions lurking just under "Is it lawful to pay taxes to Caesar or not?" are no less challenging to and testing of us today than they were to Jesus—except they are more complicated because each of us is part of what it means to be Caesar.

To be a Christian and to be a citizen simply cannot be separated. There's the rub. For us, the question could not have been more clearly put: "What is due God?" Jesus gives his ultimate answer to the Pharisees' question in two succinct commandments just a few paragraphs beyond our reading in Matthew, before the chapter ends. The familiar "Love God with your heart, soul and mind, and love your neighbor as yourself." Love of neighbor and love of God, to paraphrase Jesus' way of answering the Pharisees, are opposite sides of the same coin. It takes the whole self to worship God; it takes no less of the self to love our neighbor if we are to love her or him as we love ourselves. Probably no scripture inspires me more than those words in Genesis where heaven proclaims that we are made in the image of God. But where do most of us find that image most vividly: in our neighbor, or in our mirror? What could be more offensive to God than the phrase each of us has said or thought: "There but for the grace of God go I"? In this most individualistic of all earth's nations, "self-fulfillment" and "me first" are synonymous with "life, liberty and the pursuit of happiness." Is that all it means?

American Christianity—really American religion of any sort—is the most individualistic on earth. We Disciples of Christ are prime examples. Nobody is going to tell us what to believe. No creeds. No common statements of faith. But the challenge comes when we try to tell someone else who we are, what we think, what we affirm. On one hand, think of the problems of American Catholics. They live in a hierarchal old-European model of church, where authority from the pope on down gives them at its best a wonderful sense of community. They can go anywhere on earth and find a church with a familiar liturgy and feel at home. But in America Catholics are, from my point of view, rightly bristling, especially so with the latest encyclical on morality that continues absolutely to forbid good people's responsible practice of contraception or abortion, and to deny others' humanity with their proscription of homosexuality. American Catholic individualism is a needed corrective to absolutism in community life. But on the other hand, we Protestants, basking in our individuality, cannot seem to hold on to our communities. Denominations continue to crop up—scores more in the last two years. Denominations split, the most recent the Southern Baptists, and some prophets are all but taking bets that we Disciples will break up for the fourth time before the end of the century. When people don't like something about the church to which they belong, they vote with their feet. Their sense of community is rarely more important than their concern for their own individuality. Such an approach to life is killing American ecumenism. What is due God? Here's the American way: Love God as I see God. Love my neighbor until we disagree. Is God due anything more?

The implications are all over the human map. Yesterday we fed lunch to nearly one hundred street people, and I suppose that's about all we can do by ourselves to love our hungry neighbors. But what about the street called Park Avenue, where some of our neighbors literally control billions and homeless, sick people sleep on our steps? What is due God? You shall love your neighbor as yourself.

To whom are we giving, Caesar or God, when our government proposes to develop a health-care program that will provide benefits to the 22 million people now tragically denied adequate medical services? Or is the question, How much will it cost me? What is due God? You shall love your neighbor as yourself.

We are the lowest-taxed nation of all earth's democracies. Also, we give the most to churches and charities of all earth's democracies. Yet of all earth's first-world democracies we have more homeless and hungry than any. This metropolis has a higher infant-mortality rate than rural India. I believe underneath each of these facts lurks the question of what is God's and what is Caesar's. The questions we face when we vote in political elections or pledge in church stewardship programs are exactly the same. How is my life—what I give, what I'm taxed, what I do—an example of loving God and neighbor?

We are a nation dedicated to the individual's rights—personal rights, economic rights, property rights, religious rights. None of us would want to give up any of these. But we also are children of God, who calls us to community, to be Christ's living body in the world. Individuals who cherish their rights while denying their neighbors' needs deny Christ and defeat the strength of the nation they claim to love. So to the question, "What is Caesar's and what is God's?" I don't know any answer except: *it's all God's anyway*. None of it is mine. What kind of steward am I—I, individual...I, citizen...I, Christian...I, neighbor? The response we make to one of those "I's," I suspect, is the answer we make to all of them.

$\mathcal{K}$EEP THE FAITH, TELL THE STORY

Roy L. Griggs

> *Congregations often lose sight of their purpose for being.*
> *Many activities confuse and cause one to lose focus.*
> *This sermon is a good example of clarification of the*
> *importance of holding on and letting go.*
> *Challenging and stimulating!*

1 Thessalonians 2:13–17; Matthew 28:16–20

One of my most influential mentors in the Christian ministry was Dr. Kenneth Kuntz, long-time pastor of First Christian Church in Hannibal, Missouri. During his seventeen-year tenure in that pulpit he gave strong leadership to my home congregation.

Following two long Missouri pastorates, he went on to become president of the Division of Homeland Ministries of the Christian Church (Disciples of Christ) in Indianapolis. His creative leadership there soon overshadowed his days as a pastoral minister. However, some of us will always remember him in the pulpit, at the hospital, or as one simply giving guidance to some of us who were beginning the journey through college and seminary.

Kenneth was not always easy to get along with. He was, at times, a stubborn Prussian. But those of us who knew him over the years were far more impressed with his warm and vulnerable side. He was a pastor at heart, and somehow the bureaucracy could never quite efface that instinct.

He was a man who called a spade a spade. As a college student I was invited by the Christian Women's Fellowship to speak at one of their banquets. They wanted to see how I, as a Timothy of the congregation, was progressing in my preparation for the ministry. After the talk the usual number of nice

---

Roy Griggs is senior pastor of First Christian Church in Tulsa, Oklahoma.

ladies came up and affectionately gave appreciative comments. Afterwards Kenneth called me to his study, shut the door, and said, "You didn't put much time into preparing that talk, did you?" He was right. But he taught me a lesson. I have never given a talk since that time without adequate preparation.

One of Kenneth's favorite remarks was, "Keep the faith, tell the story!" His late wife, Ruth, once told me that she was sometimes irritated because he used that phrase so often.

Kenneth died of cancer several years ago. Ruth told me that his last days were spent in the comforts of their home. They knew his time was brief and made the most of it. She said that shortly before his death, as they were wheeling him out of the house to place him in the ambulance for the trip to the hospital, he looked up at her and said his last words. You guessed it: "Keep the faith, tell the story!"

Those were not random words. They reflected the faith journey of a great Christian over a distinguished forty-year ministry. They were the culmination of the spiritual search, the biblical study, and the intellectual grappling with the great precepts of the Christian faith. These words represent the fundamental task and unique opportunity of Christianity in any generation.

Because of Kenneth Kuntz, and a host of others across the centuries who believed in them, we are called to face the implications of these words for our lives: "Keep the faith, tell the story!"

In a sense, these two phrases are like Siamese twins. We cannot have one without the other. Keeping the faith means to tell the story. To tell the story is a part of keeping the faith. However, let's look at them separately.

I. "Keep the Faith"

Every generation for two thousand years has been handed this challenge. In a time when there are so many faiths competing for our loyalty, we need to hear this. What does it mean to "keep the faith"?

Paul faces this in his second letter to the Thessalonians. He writes, "So then, brothers and sisters, stand firm and hold fast to the traditions that you were taught by us, either by word of mouth or by our letter." (2:15.)

Verse 15 is a part of a larger section from verses 13–15 in which Paul gives us his theology in a nutshell.

> A. The greatness and love of God
> B. The glory of our Lord Jesus Christ
> C. The power of the gospel preaching

Every Sunday when we gather in this sanctuary, we lift up these three things. They are the focus of our faith.

We focus our attention on the glory of Jesus. The great artists, philosophers, and scientists have brought us light and truth. We owe them a debt we can never repay. But none of them has given us what Jesus has—a system of true values that has enabled us to live and die in peace. In addition, he has provided a spiritual power that enables us to resist temptation and to grow in self-control and generosity. Jesus has given us all these things as a part of our faith.

Paul has forced us back to our beginnings, our point of origin. He has prompted us to ask the big questions: Who am I? From whence did I come? Where am I going? What is my purpose? Is there One beyond?

When we say, "Keep the faith," we are talking about the whole story of God's love, Jesus' life and ministry, and the work of the Holy Spirit.

You see, we are the keepers! All of this is just one generation from disappearing. If we do not keep it in our hearts, our families, our churches, then the next generation will never find the salvation we have cherished and offered to others.

II. "Tell the Story"

But this is only half of our task. Certainly we must "keep the faith," but we must also "tell the story." What is the story? It is, again, "the greatness and love of God and the glory of our Lord Jesus Christ."

Here Paul makes his third point. It concerns the power of gospel preaching. In 2:15 we read, "Stand firm and hold fast to the traditions...taught by us, either by word of mouth or by our letter." Verse 14 says, "For this purpose he called you through our proclaimation of the good news, so that you may obtain the glory of our Lord Jesus Christ."

There is an indescribable power in preaching. There are Sundays when I feel it strongly! It exists at times quite apart from the congregation and preacher. It is almost a third entity at work in our midst. It is the Holy Spirit moving among us to call us to action, converting us from our sins and inspiring us to give ourselves to that which is beyond ourselves. At its best it is the proclamation of the love of God for all, regardless of race, class, religion, gender, or sexual orientation.

There is also an indescribable power in great Christian living. Who said, "I would rather see a sermon than hear one"? When we commit ourselves to "the greatness of God and love of God and the glory of our Lord Jesus Christ," we preach a powerful sermon that the world needs to hear.

The last thing that Jesus said on this earth was "Tell the story!" In our second scripture reading, Jesus gathers with his disciples on the mountaintop, and there he gives them his parting words. We believe these to be among his greatest. They have been called the Great Commission: "Go therefore and make disciples of all nations, baptizing them in the name of the Father and of the Son and of the Holy Spirit, and teaching them to obey everything that I have commanded you. And remember, I am with you always, to the end of the age" (Matthew 28:19–20).

We have entered into a disappointing time in the history of the church. We are doing a better job of keeping the faith than we are of telling the story!

There is a heresy rampant in the world today. It says, "I can keep my faith for myself. My religion is personal. I don't need the church, the body of Christ. I don't need other Christians, my brothers and sisters who are also trying to find the better life. I will just hold onto and keep my faith for myself alone!"

That can be selfish religion! Jesus has given us the responsibility to help one another grow in the faith journey. There is no such thing as solitary Christianity!

This same attitude can be seen on the next level, that of the congregation. We somehow think that Christianity can be lived out solely as a local church. Year by year our vision grows smaller in terms of Jesus' Great Commission. More and more we are taking care of local concerns and forgetting that there is no such thing as a "local" Christian church.

We are a part of the body of Christ that stretches across the entire globe. We are called to tell the story to all people in every land! Could we say it better than Stephen Vincent Benet?

> God pity us indeed, for we are human
>   And do not always see
> The vision when it comes, the shining change.
>   Or if we see it, do not follow it.
> Because it is too hard, too strange, too new,
>   Too unbelievable, too difficult,
> Warring too much with common, easy ways...
>   Life is not lost by dying! Life is lost
> Minute by minute, day by dragging day,
>   In a thousand small, undaring ways...
> Always, and always, life can be
>   Lost by not daring, willing, going on
> Beyond the ragged edge of fortitude
>   To something more...something no man has seen.

How pathetic it would be if the history of the church in this century ended with the indictment that it had reduced itself to these words: "small, undaring, selfish...."

Keep the faith. Tell the story.

How are we doing? Next week is Consecration Sunday. We will have a real measuring stick as we bring our commitments to this chancel and get ready for another year of witness and work. We are getting ready for another year of keeping the faith and telling the story:

> As we build a stronger family program for young adults, youth, and children.
>
> As we perpetuate our senior adult program, one of the finest in the state.
>
> As we continue to build one of the finest music programs in this city.
>
> As we maintain one of the most beautiful facilities in this community.
>
> As we feed the hungry, educate the ignorant, and care for the homeless.
>
> As we reach out across the world and carry out the Great Commission, bringing others to a saving knowledge of Jesus.

Consecration Sunday poses a crucial question: "How well will we 'keep the faith and tell the story' in this next year?"

Next Sunday as we share in an act of commitment, the bringing forward of our estimates of giving, we will be surrounded by a host of others who want us to be the most faithful congregation possible as we move through the last decade of the twentieth century. So thanks, Kenneth Kuntz, for sharing a little of your life with us this morning. Thanks, Gaines Cook, Dale Fiers, Mae Yoho Ward, and thousands of pastors, Christian educators, and other professional and lay church workers who have given their lives to keeping the faith and telling the story.

With God's help, we will do the same!

Let us pray: Loving God, we thank you for all of those women and men of faith upon whose shoulders we stand. Grant that we may faithfully carry on the great procession across the centuries and rightfully represent you in our day. We give you our lives and ask only that you will use us for your purposes. In Jesus' name. Amen.

COMPASSION, PATIENCE, AND THE WOMB OF GOD

Ron M. Zorn

> *To communicate grace in this world sometimes requires*
> *that we break open old images with new metaphors.*
> *"The womb of God contains all us bastards." This is*
> *the essence of grace that keeps us giving. This*
> *sermon is worth some thoughtful reflection as a*
> *model for effective preaching about stewardship.*

Perhaps one of the most difficult fruits of the Spirit for me to receive is patience. Like most people, I am most impatient with myself. I expect too much of my life, my vocation, and my development. My compromised discipleship, my petty concerns, my hesitancy to have my day's carefully planned agenda interrupted by the unforeseen, and a host of other failings remind me that time is running out if I am to be shaped by the Spirit of my Lord. And the people who mean the most to me, my wife and daughter, are too often the recipients of the accumulated frustrations of "a candle burning at both ends." Despite what I know about holistic health and how I counsel my parishioners, the ability to forgive and accept myself in the context of patient love is a difficult grace for me to practice.

From what has been written above, one would not be surprised to discover that I also find myself impatient with others. Why this universal obsession with the trivial, the nonessential, the mundane? In a world with so many wounds, why must I hear words such as nigger, fag, wetback, and kike? Didn't we learn anything from Auschwitz and Selma about the dangers of prejudice and intolerance? And in a world of hunger and poverty, why must we continue to live as though life *does* consist in the abundance of possessions? Has it occurred to anyone (certainly not to any politician!) that the current crisis in

Ron M. Zorn is minister of the Wabash Christian Church in Wabash, Indiana.

"family values" is deeply rooted in what we as a society value most—money, money, money? Sometimes I find myself agreeing with an old seminary friend who said the time is fast approaching when it will be easier to lock up all the sane persons and let the insane have their way with the world.

And then I find myself impatient with the church. Two thousand years of Christianity should have moved us farther down the road to the Peaceable Realm. Splintered into denominations, the body of Christ, as Bill Nichols has said, is broken not *for* us but *by* us. We claim to be saved by grace and then return to the same old legalistic spirit when it suits our purposes and our prejudices, as we exclude others from the grace of God. We seem to be guided more by what is expedient than what is faithful. Rarely do churches make monumental decisions involving major expenditures of money, time, and commitment with a reckless trust in the will of God as revealed in the life of our Lord. Instead of walking the pilgrim trail of faithful discipleship, we have often chosen to homestead on the Plain called Ease and to tarry at Vanity Fair.

So what can I (we?) do with all this impatience? Sometimes, I feel that a little impatience is not so bad. Perhaps it even reflects the divine impatience God must feel with this wayward creation. Righteous indignation has served many a good cause in the history of humanity. And in a world with hundreds of millions of starving, burning, suffering, and abused children, anyone who cannot be righteously indignant knows precious little about the God of Jesus Christ. Nevertheless, perpetual or even predominant impatience is an unhealthy and ultimately damaging way to approach self, world, and church.

It helps us to remember that the words "compassion" and "patience" have their origins in the Latin word for suffering, *pati*. We ordinarily think of compassion as the ability to identify with another's suffering and to enter into solidarity with that person's lot in life. We think of compassion for the sick, the poor, the hungry, the oppressed, the wounded in life. Certainly, such compassion is well-documented in the Bible, both on God's part and that of God's faithful servants. And heaven knows the need for such compassion in our kind of world. But perhaps we should also think of compassion in terms of God's patience with us in our stubbornness, prejudice, fears, stumbling, and underdeveloped consciences.

Will Campbell, in his autobiographical *Brother To A Dragonfly,* tells of a conversation he once had with his friend

P. D. East, when they had enjoyed a little too much of the fruit of the vine. East offered this challenge: "In one sentence, tell me the essence of Christianity." Campbell's reply surprised even himself: "We're all bastards, but God loves us anyway."

Sometime later, one of Campbell's best friends was shot in cold blood by a deputy sheriff in a Southern community, simply for being with an African American in a local store. This friend was one of the finest, most loving and gentle human beings Campbell had ever known. And he grieved his loss deeply. Campbell knew that the Southern courts would not pursue justice during those dark days of the early civil rights movement. Once again, Campbell found himself with his friend, P. D. East. And as they shared a bottle, East asked Campbell if he still believed the essence of "Mr. Jesus' " message was, "We're all bastards, but God loves us anyway." Campbell replied that that was still his conviction. And then East asked, "You mean that you believe that God loves that deputy sheriff as much as the kindest, gentlest man either of us has ever known?"

Campbell's tears began to flow. He said for the first time in his life he had heard the gospel in the core of his being. He knew that if his definition of the essence of Christianity were not true, then there was no gospel—no gospel for the deputy sheriff, for the lost friend who would have been the first to embrace the definition, or for himself. And from that moment on, Campbell began to have compassion (patience?) for all of God's children—the oppressed African American and the "white trash" who contributed to that oppression, the poor who suffered from others' greed, and the greedy who suffered from the emptiness of their twisted lives.

Reflecting upon this incident, I find great comfort in the words of the psalmist: "[God] does not deal with us according to our sins…As a father has compassion for his children, so the LORD has compassion on those who fear him. For he knows how we were made; he remembers that we are dust"(Psalm 103:10, 13–14). The root of the Hebrew word for "compassion" is most interesting. That root means *womb*. Originally, compassion referred to the deep love and empathy a mother has for her children and the accompanying love and empathy experienced by those who have shared the same womb. Although the psalmist refers to God as *father*, the deeper background for compassion is the womb of a mother. And in a real sense, we have all shared the womb of God. Prior to the sins that make us all "bastards" is the divine womb that envelops us all and affirms us as God's children.

The New Testament scholar Marcus Borg, in his *Jesus: A New Vision,* shows how Jesus ascribed to God the quality of compassion before all others. Borg argues that Jesus replaced the Holiness code admonition, "You must be holy just as God is holy," with the Kingdom code, "You must be compassionate just as your heavenly Father is compassionate." In Jesus' day, much of society was determined by that holiness orientation, which, of course, led to impatience with those who were not "holy." But where the emphasis on holiness excluded many, Jesus' focus on compassion embraced all: The womb that envelops us is stronger and greater than our sin or even justifiable divine impatience.

A far greater connection exists between compassion and patience than merely a shared etymological root. And the realization and celebration of that connection deep in the womb of God may have far more to do with my discipleship than I ordinarily assume. If I am to benefit from God's patience, then I must allow myself, others, and the church to benefit not only from heaven's patience but from my own. For after all, we share the same womb. My suspicion is that I may not be alone in the need to plumb the depths of God's compassion.

$\mathcal{A}$ Nice, Clear Command

Charles D. Watkins

Tithing is hard to preach about. This sermon will help. It acknowledges the modern questions about tithing and yet holds it up as an appropriate way to respond to the love that God has for us.

There are a good many days when I wish that Jesus had taken his disciples aside one afternoon and said to them, "Now look. My work, our work—God's work—is important, the most important work in the world. So from now on, tell anybody who wants to be a follower of mine to set aside the first tenth of their income for my work in the world." A nice, clear command.

If Jesus had done that, and if we all obeyed that command, then our church would receive nearly $2,000,000 this year, assuming we all gave one-tenth of our income after taxes. There would be no need for a stewardship campaign or for next spring's capital campaign. We'd just all do what Jesus said to do—we'd give our tenth, and our church would receive more than twice as much as the current expense, missions, and capital budgets are now. We could double or triple our mission outreach, add more staff, and do whatever we thought we needed to do to our facilities. It's so simple, so efficient, and so effective, that I just wish that Jesus had said to us, "Do this, this way, one-tenth, the first tenth for my work." A nice, clear command.

Unfortunately, Jesus did not give this commandment. And what's worse, Jesus ridiculed some of the pious folk who did give one-tenth of everything according to the law of Moses. The Pharisees were so religious, so devout, so devoted to the

---

Charles Watkins is senior pastor of Central Christian Church in Decatur, Illinois.

law, some say, that they would go out to their herb gardens where they grew mint for Derby parties and dill for their hamburgers and cumin seeds for their hamburger buns, and they'd count leaves and seed pods so that they could give every tenth one to the Lord.

After all, they reasoned, the law requires that the first tenth of the harvest is for the Lord—grain, wine, oil, and firstlings of the flock. So they were just being meticulous about ensuring that the first tenth of the harvest of their herb gardens was dutifully tithed as well.

But Jesus said, "Woe to you, scribes and Pharisees, hypocrites! For you tithe mint, dill, and cumin, and have neglected the weightier matters of the law: justice and mercy and faith. It is these you ought to have practiced without neglecting the others. You blind guides! You strain out a gnat but swallow a camel!"(Matthew 23:23–24).

I would have liked it a lot better if Jesus had called those names and then said, "But at least you are careful tithers, and I commend you for that, God love you." But Jesus didn't. The brighter side, of course, is that Jesus never forbade tithing, never said tithing was a bad idea. And most probably he assumed that everybody listening to him was already a steady tither, since it was the law, after all.

Jesus didn't say anything bad about tithing, except that tithers have no excuse for overlooking the more important parts of the law, like justice and mercy and faith. He probably did not want us to lose our perspective on what is vital, and he certainly didn't want us preening like the Pharisees saying, "Look at me, how good I am. I tithe on every little thing, even mint leaves. Am I not wonderful, and don't you wish you were as good as I am?" Jesus had no patience with any kind of self-righteousness and would not tolerate any self-congratulation about how good we are for obeying the law and doing what God expects.

Jesus told another story, about a Pharisee who went into the temple to pray. The Pharisee stood by himself and prayed thus, "God, I thank thee that I am not like other men, extortioners, unjust, adulterers, or even like this miserable tax collector over here. I fast twice a week, I give tithes of all that I get. Am I not wonderful? Am I not righteous? Aren't you just proud to death over me, Lord? Gosh, I'm good!"

But the despised tax collector—and he really was a cheating, stealing scoundrel, traitor to his own people—would not even lift up his eyes to heaven but beat his breast, saying,

"God be merciful to me, a sinner!" Then Jesus said, "I tell you, this man went down to his home justified rather than the other; for all who exalt themselves will be humbled, but all who humble themselves will be exalted"(see Luke 18:10–10).

Once again, more harsh words for a good tither. But notice that it's not the tithing that Jesus condemns. It's our attitudes about our good habits that he can't stand. It's our thinking that we are so great just because we do what we're supposed to do.

Still, it would really help on a day like today if Jesus could have come up with just a few kind words for tithers and maybe just one nice, clear, understated command like, "Of course, you will tithe on earned income, interest, dividends, and capital gains after paying all state, local, and federal taxes, except in years when you experience windfall profits, and in those years you will, naturally, give a double tithe. And by the way, remember the church in your will." Just a nice, clear command.

Of course, the reason I wish Jesus had given such a command is that if he had, then the church would never have to hold out its tin cup and ask people to contribute. So much really bad religion in our culture is so completely focused on money that it makes us in our church want to go to the other extreme, as if to say, "Money? Oh, yes, filthy lucre. I suppose some of that will be necessary this year, if anybody thinks of dropping some in the plate."

You see, we are so anxious in our church not to be money-grubbing and dollar-focused, that we won't even go to one another, except under duress, and say, "Hey! You need to give more to the church. Come on, ante up, let's go. You know we've got duct tape holding the carpeting together down there. You ought to be good for fifteen per cent more this year at least."

Do you see, since we can't run a church without money, and we really hate to ask each other for it, wouldn't it have been a lot better if Jesus could have brought himself on some occasion to give one nice, clear command in favor of tithing that would solve all our financial problems? What a great help that would have been!

So why didn't Jesus do that? Well, there are several possibilities. One is that it had already been done. Tithing had been part of God's law for over a thousand years, and maybe it never even entered Jesus' mind that God's people would not always give the first tenth of everything for God's work. Maybe he just assumed that that was how it had always been and always would be. Some churches that are a lot more successful at motivating giving than we are believe that this is the case. Tithing was God's law, and Jesus did not come to take away even a jot or a tittle from that law. He just assumed it.

A second reason that Jesus might have had for not specifying what we are to give for his work might be his desire to remove from us any temptation toward self-righteousness and self-satisfaction. He may have thought our spiritual health would be better if we could never, ever stand before God and say, "See, Lord, how good and generous I am?" By leaving vague just how much is enough to give, Jesus takes both the floor and the ceiling off our giving. If I am giving 10 percent easily, out of habit, then maybe I ought really to be giving 15 or 20 percent.

A third reason that Jesus might have had for not telling us what to give could have been a belief that ten percent was not the issue, that actually one hundred percent of what we receive belongs to God. It's all the Lord's. To talk about ten percent belonging to God and ninety percent belonging to me is blasphemy. It's not the Lord's share and my share, because it's all God's money, every last penny. Maybe Jesus wanted us to consider how much we dare take out of God's money to live on this year and how much of God's money can be used to do God's work in the world.

A fourth reason that Jesus might have had for not directing our giving may have been that he wanted us to give out of love and devotion, and not out of duty. Maybe God wants us to give because we love the Lord, not because of fear, not because of guilt, and not because Jesus told us what to give in a nice, clear command.

You know, when my birthday's coming up, I don't take my son aside and say to him, "Hey, my special day is coming up, so be sure to start setting aside about $2.50 a week out of your allowance so that you can get a nice gift to honor me with. Make it about $25 this year, and make sure it's something I like."

You don't say that to your child either, and maybe God would not say such a thing to us. Maybe as the Lord's special day approaches each week, God would prefer us to think about what our love calls us to do for the most important person in our lives, the Lord.

There could be a good many other reasons that Jesus did not give us a nice, clear command about what we should contribute to his cause. And among those might be a desire that preachers and churches humble themselves from time to time and get out their tin cups and ask folks to please give.

But despite what I wish Jesus had done, what he in truth did do was to put our giving on a new plane above and beyond any commandment or law. He claimed everything, all our possessions and all our income. And then he called on us to love the Lord our God with all our heart and soul and mind and strength, and our neighbor as ourselves. And then after he was no longer among us, those who followed him established the church to carry on his work and proclaim his message of salvation to all people.

As you fill out your giving card, what you put down is a matter primarily between you and the Lord. I hope that you will love God and honor God in your giving, that you will put God first. The good Lord probably does not care nearly as much about what our church budget is as the Lord cares about your relationship with God, about the quality of your commitment to God's cause in the world, about the spirit in which you give to God's church some of the Lord's money which has been entrusted to you as servant and steward. Do your best today to show your true love of God and to honor the Lord. By your generosity, prove that you don't need a nice, clear commandment.

$\mathcal{T}$HE SACRAMENTAL $\mathcal{T}$ITHE

Ronald J. Allen

Confessing confusion about tithing, this sermon lays groundwork for clarification. A biblical exegesis reveals tithing in a fresh new light. This sermon is full of ideas that could be developed in a series of stewardship sermons.

Deuteronomy 14:22–29

I must confess that I have never before preached on tithing. I ask myself, Why? Why have you reached middle age and have never preached on this subject that so permeates the Bible? As I think about this question, I realize that I have been uncomfortable with the understandings of tithing that have unfolded in my own mind. At different times, I have had different understandings of tithing, and I have not been comfortable with any of them. I wonder, is this true for you, too?

For a long time, I thought of the tithe as a work that people could do in order to earn God's favor. I pictured humorless Hebrews laying their tithes on the altar with tired faces and bent backs; they look up at God with pleading eyes. "Is ten percent enough?" I wondered if some of the deacons felt the same way as they carried those heavy brass offering trays down the center aisle on the Doxology.

I was fortunate on half of this score. Our Sunday school teachers taught grace. God loves us and accepts us because of God's unmerited favor. They made sure that we knew that we

Ron Allen is associate professor of preaching and New Testament at Christian Theological Seminary in Indianapolis, Indiana. He is the author or co-author of numerous books on preaching, including *A Credible and Timely Word* (Chalice Press) and *The Teaching Sermon*.

could not earn our way into God's circle of friends. There was "all-sufficient grace even for me." This was a relief to a boy who needed all of his allowance to go to the movies *and* get malt balls.

It was many years before someone corrected the second half of this score. You see, I thought that the Jewish people believed in earning their way into God's favor. And what easier way to buy a quart of divine love than to tithe? I was quite surprised to learn that the Jewish people do not regard the tithe as a way of buying off God. They, too, teach that we are saved by grace. In fact, one of their rabbis, commenting on a psalm and speaking for many others, says to God, "'Deal with thy servant according to the *hesed* (grace)' (Psalm 119:124). Perhaps thou hast pleasure in our good works? Merit and good works we have not; act toward us in *hesed*."[1] But if a tithe is not a merit, what is it?

In a related mode, I thought of tithing as paying what I owe. We paid for food from Piggy Hogg's supermarket. We paid Dr. Parker when I was sick. Ten percent was God's monthly bill, much like the house payment. I don't remember thinking it at the time, but it would be normal to wonder if God would evict us for nonpayment.

I was happier with another notion of tithing. I would not have put it this crudely, but for a while I thought that tithing was a business deal with God. I give God 10 percent. And God agrees to bless me. Tithing was an opportunity to put my money with the Divine Investment Counselor. And not just my money but my whole life. If I tithed, I could expect happiness in every arena.

But empirical observation got in the way. I tuned into this channel of thought about the time I was a sophomore in high school. So I tried tithing. But the first thing you know, I had to get braces on my teeth—for the *second* time. And why all this acne? But I was ashamed of these petty thoughts when I realized that one of our family friends, a lifelong tither, was dying of cancer. Okay, so maybe I misunderstood. Maybe the blessing isn't always in material goods.

The strange thing is, I don't remember ever reading what the Bible itself has to say about tithing. Not even as a young pastor when I was preaching stewardship sermons every fall. I just accepted what *other* people said *about* tithing. When I finally got around actually to reading the Bible for myself, I discovered that a lot of what people said about tithing is not in the Bible at all. And I discovered that some of what the Bible says turned my previous ideas about tithing inside out.

In the first place, the subject of tithing hardly permeates the Bible. It is mentioned a couple of times in Genesis.[2] And the practice of tithing seems to be assumed by other Jewish writers right into the period of Jesus.[3] But the Hebrew Bible contains only a handful of discussions of tithing that do more than mention the practice.[4]

Deuteronomy brings the most light to bear on tithing, and it does so in only two short passages that I read a few moments ago. Although brief, Deuteronomy's perspective on tithing is quite surprising. I have always heard tithing discussed under the rubric of give, give, give. You need to give 10 percent to God. But did you hear what Deuteronomy prescribes?

Suppose you were an Israelite. You would go into the field and gather 10 percent of the yield of your crop. And you would gather 10 percent of the firstborn from your flocks. Then you would take these things and go to the place that God chose (which refers to the temple at Jerusalem). You would prepare a festive meal from your own tithe, and you would eat the meal with your family. If you lived so far away that it would be terribly inconvenient for you to take your own food to the temple, then you could sell your tithe at your local market, and take the cash with you to Jerusalem. In Jerusalem you would buy food and prepare the meal. "And you shall eat there in the presence of the Lord your God, you and your household rejoicing together."(Deuteronomy 14:26.)

And not only that, but you invite the Levites in your town to join you. And every third year, you take the tithe and put it in the town storehouse for the Levites and for the resident aliens, the orphans, and the widows.

Now why do this? It is clear enough why you provide for the resident alien, the orphan, and the widow. The resident alien is a non-Israelite who is residing in Israel for a long period of time. That person may not have land or crops or flocks and hence may not have enough food to eat. And the same thing is true of the orphan and the widow.

Remember, one of God's greatest desires in Deuteronomy is to bless all who are in the land of Israel. And it is hard to feel blessed when you are scratching for food from day to day. Can you imagine what it would be like to wake up every morning and wonder where you would get food, for you *or* for your children? So the tithe is a way to provide food for those in the community who are at risk. God uses tithing to bless those in the community who feel least blessed.[5]

And it is clear enough why you feed the Levites. The Levites are Israel's equivalent of the associate minister. The priest is the senior minister and the Levite is the associate. So when you eat your tithe with the Levite, it is like having the associate pastor to your house to grill burgers on the deck. And the Levites tithe the tithes that they receive to the priests so that the priests can eat.[6]

The priest and the Levite have no land or crops or flocks. They work at the temple and lead religious instruction and the rest of the religious life of Israel. The tithe makes it possible for the Levite and the priest to give themselves full-time and without distraction to their work. But the tithe is more than just paying the pastor's salary and keeping the organ tuned and the gas bill paid. In Deuteronomic Israel, the temple was the symbol *par excellence* of God's love and trustworthiness. The temple was the most vivid, physical reminder that God had commanded the people to live in justice and love with one another by following the commandments. The temple and religious teachings and rites were concrete reminders of the covenant between God and Israel. The tithe was a way of keeping these realities alive at the center of Israel's consciousness.

When you tithe, you say "Yes" to God. You say, "I accept your love for me and for all. I intend to manifest that love in all my relationships."

But why do you eat your own tithe? I thought the tithe was something to give away. But Deuteronomy is very clear that you prepare a meal and eat it with your family and that you rejoice in the eating.

If we had been reading Deuteronomy from start to finish, we would know how to answer this question. Deuteronomy is manic on idolatry. In the chapter just before our reading, the text says that if anyone attempts to lead you into idolatry, "you must not yield to or heed any such persons. Show them no pity or compassion and do not shield them. But you shall surely kill them" (13:8–9). Now, today we would say that is an extreme in the extreme. It is hardly the will of the God of unconditional love to flatten idolaters like flies against the wallpaper. But this commandment impresses on the reader the necessity of avoiding idolatry.

But again I ask, why? Why this concern about idolatry? Because idolatry is a mistake. In idolatry you mistake that which is finite and relative for God, who is infinite and transcendent. You mistake a little bit of creation for the Creator.

And more. God wants to bless the people. When the people are obedient, God blesses them. But when they are disobedient, God curses them. And blessing includes fertility in the soil and abundant food and healthy flocks. But when the people are disobedient, the curse falls upon them, and the curse includes drought and shrivelled crops and long, hungry winters (chs. 27—28). Like acid on glass, Deuteronomy aims to etch this fact into the hearts and minds of the Israelites: God is the source of your blessing; idolatry leads to the curse.

Oh, but the idols are so tempting. You can see an idol. An Israelite could have a longing, or a need, or he might be in trouble. The Israelite could not see God. But there was the idol in its stone splendor. Instant gratification.

Do you understand that? I do. I have a restlessness in my soul. I want something. I cannot name it, but I can feel it. I want more to my life than I have. And every seven minutes, the television shows me things I can buy to fulfill my longing. I would rather run to the mall and put my fulfillment on my Visa card than struggle in a moldy church basement with people I hardly know gathered around a book whose last words were written two thousand years ago in search of a God whom I cannot see. As a pastor, how many times have I drawn back from witness by saying, "The congregation just isn't ready for it yet"? I have a lifestyle to support and five children to put through college. I cannot tithe at this point in my life. I understand why idolatry is attractive. How about you?

So how does the tithe get into this picture? God promises that if the people turn away from the idols and cleave to God, God will bless them. And the eating of the tithe is part of the proof. When you eat the tithe, you taste the trustworthiness of God. In your hands, you hold a sign of God's power and will to bless. And as you pass the burgers to the Levite, you remember that God has provided the means to help you to be continually blessed. And as you take your tithes to the storehouse, you remember not only that God wants to bless the alien, the orphan and the widow, but that you are linked in blessing to them.

The tithe is not so much something we give to God. It is a sacrament that God gives us.

But questions come up. Is a tithe on gross or is it on net? Israel did not have a precise parallel to the categories of gross and net. I cannot casually say one or the other. Today we pay taxes to the secular government. Some of our taxes help orphans and widows (symbolically speaking), much like the tithe

in Israel. Today's orphan and widow do not rely on the church
for support in the same way that they relied on the tithe in
Deuteronomic Israel.

You could make the case that a part of a contemporary
tithe is administered through the programs of our governments
that aim to help people in the Deuteronomic way. In fact, I
read about people who calculate the percentage of their taxes
that go to bless people. They pay those taxes and withhold the
rest. Particularly they withhold the telephone tax, since that
goes directly to preparation for war. This, however, is not as
easy as it may seem. Can you always draw a neat, clean line
between a government expenditure that helps people and one
that does not?

I think there is a good reason for tithing, even when some
of our tax dollars address the Deuteronomic concern for human welfare. I have not seen this in a scholarly publication,
but I believe there is something deeply symbolic about offering 10 percent of your life resources to God. The Israelites were
not the only peoples of antiquity to practice tithing. Tithing
was a common feature of the religious life of many ancient
peoples.[7]

I am not suggesting that the tithe is a Jungian-like arche-
type. I am reporting that a lot of people in history have found
that the practice of tithing is a fundamental way of acknowl-
edging their connection to ultimate reality. I believe that when
we tithe, the deepest parts of ourselves are stirred to say "Yes"
to God.

Furthermore, the Israelites lived in an agricultural
economy. They could eat their tithes. The taste of leeks and
fresh-baked bread is the taste of providence. Few of us raise
our own tithes. But by the time of Jesus, the rabbis of Israel
had concluded that a tithe could be money. And the early Christians quickly joined them. We cannot eat our money. But when
we tithe, we receive signs of God's providence. They may not
be material signs; but they are signs that God is ever with us,
feeling our pain, intensifying our joy, working ever for our good.

Doesn't everyone receive such signs? Sure. Tithing does
not increase God's will to bless us by even one tiny decimal
point. God's unconditional love is poured out evenly, like the
ribbon of cement that makes a highway. Unconditional means
unconditional. Tithing does not create a condition whereby you
get more love. But if my point is correct about the tithe being
a symbol that touches us at the deepest levels of the self, then
it stands to reason that tithing could help us be more aware of

God's omnipresence. And sometimes you can feel that presence as surely as you can taste the bread and cup.

I know. I know. No guarantees. Sometimes we can put out so much static that the screen of God's presence is completely fuzzy. But I think that tithing helps our antennae pick up the signal that is always beaming towards us.

I remember a friend who was about sixty years old when a bad thing happened. As you can guess, he was a lifelong tither. He was a materials manager for a hospital, which means he ordered all the stuff that hospitals use, except for the medicines. About a year before, he had been living his dream life in California. He had been to California in World War II and had felt that he was as close to paradise as he would get in North America. Throughout his adult life, he wanted to return there, but family circumstances had conspired against him until he was about fifty-five and became materials manager of a hospital in southern California. He felt as blessed as blessed could be.

His mother, however, still lived in the Midwest, and when her health failed, he needed to return to look after her. A hospital in our community hired him. His first job was to organize the move of the hospital from its old building to a new one, a mammoth effort that required six months of long hours of careful planning. It went off without a hitch. People who observed it said it was the most impressive move for a hospital of that size they had ever seen.

He settled in for the last five years of his working life until retirement. Then, one day, out of the blue, the hospital decided they could not afford his salary. Where do you go and what do you do when you're sixty years old and your geographical mobility is extremely limited and there aren't any job openings in your field? Well, you get angry and depressed. But if you're this guy, you work through it. The church community rallied around him. He went to work for a hardware store, and he set up a bookkeeping business in his basement. But he never stopped tithing.

After things had settled down, and the spark had come back to his eyes, I asked him, "How did you get through it?" He said it was tough, the toughest thing he had ever faced. The indignity. The injustice. The impotence. The economic fear. The feeling of shame in the presence of his family and friends. But one thing he knew: God was with him. Even with God, in these circumstances, all things might not be possible. But it was certainly possible to live with dignity and creativity. "And besides," he said, "look at me. Working at the store I've lost thirty pounds, and I'll probably have thirty years longer to enjoy my wife and kids."

Would God have been any less present if he had never given God a penny? No. But a life of tithing had helped him become aware of God's presence.

And the same thing can be true for you and me. Tithing is a gift from God to help us. And it helps the church and the aliens and orphans and widows of our world. What about it? Will you accept this gift?

---

[1] Cited in C.G. Montefiore and H. Lowe, *A Rabbinic Anthology* (New York: Schocken Books, 1974), p. 91.

[2] Genesis 14:17–20, 28:18–22. J. Christian Wilson gives a concise history of the practice of tithing in Israel in "Tithe," *The Anchor Bible Dictionary,* edited by David Noel Freedman, et. al. (New York: Doubleday, 1992) vol. 6, pp. 578-580.

[3] E.g., Amos 4:4, Nehemiah 10:37–38, II Chronicles 31:5–6, Sirach 35:11, Tobit 1:6, Judith 11:13, 1 Maccabees 3:49, 10:31, 11:35, Matthew 23:23, Luke 11:42.

[4] Leviticus 27:30–33, Numbers 18:21–32, Deuteronomy 14:22–27, 26:12–15, Malachi 3:8–10.

[5] Many of us, schooled in systems analysis, will rightly complain, "But this aspect of tithing does nothing to change the social system that creates the vulnerability of resident alien, orphan, and widow." And that is true. But it is important for us to remember that the Deuteronomic theologians did not think in terms of contemporary systems analysis. The deep concern of the text is to testify to God's desire to bless *all*. Everyone is to be included in the embrace of God's love and justice. When we today change the systems that create vulnerability, we are simply specifying the intent of the Deuteronomic concern for our world.

[6] Numbers 18:25–32, esp. v. 28.

[7] See, e.g., Terzo Natalini, *A Historical Essay on Tithes: A Collection of Sources and Texts* (Rome: Natalini, 1973), pp. 1–10.

ROBBERY WITHOUT A WEAPON

Alvin O. Jackson

*This sermon is a creative challenge to the modern desire to
control what the God of community is to control. To tithe to
the treasury is to be used to bring healing in God's name.
For people who worship at the altar of individualism and
self-fulfillment, this sermon is a powerful witness to
wholeness in giving to the community of Christ. We need
more courageous challenges such as this.*

Malachi 3:7–12*

Have you heard that on January 16, 1994, at 70 North
Bellevue, the Mississippi Boulevard Christian Church, Memphis,
Tennessee, around 11:30 a.m., a robbery was committed? An un-
determined amount of money was stolen. This doesn't appear to
be the first time that this crime was committed. The evidence
strongly suggests that this is only one of many unchecked of-
fenses that have been going on over a long period of time. The
evidence also suggests that it was an inside job. There were no
signs of forced entry. Thirty-five hundred people were present at
the scene of the crime, and at least three thousand are suspected
of actively participating in the robbery. None of the suspects has
been apprehended. The authorities are still investigating.

One of the authorities commented that in all his years of
investigating robberies, he has never seen anything like this
one before. A large sum of money was missing, but no money
seems to have changed hands. The money appears to have been
stolen from God...address unknown. No indication of weapons
used and no visible signs of a struggle. It appears to have been
a robbery without a weapon.

---

*The scripture references in this sermon are from the King James Version of the Bible.

Alvin Jackson is senior pastor of Mississippi Boulevard Christian Church in Memphis,
Tennessee—now the largest congregation of the Christian Church (Disciples of Christ),
with over 9000 members.

I have just come today on behalf of the authorities to issue the warrants for arrest. But I have also come to announce that the judge in the case, who is also God, is willing to suspend the sentences and pardon all who will make a vow never to commit this crime again.

This is the message that the prophet Malachi delivers to the people of Israel. We find in the book of Malachi that the prophet goes to the people in God's behalf. He is pleading with the people to return to God what they have taken from Him. He reads God's love letter to them, expressing the pain of God's unrequited love. He says the Lord says: "I have loved you; I have delivered you; I am your parent; I am your partner; I entered into covenant with you; I married you. You became my people and I became your God, your companion, your keeper and provider, and yet you have despised me and dishonored me and withheld yourselves, your service, and your substance from me who withholds nothing from you."

The relationship has been one-sided, and one-sided relationships just don't work. We need to do all we can from our side and on our part to keep open the channels between us and God. Healthy relationships cannot be one-sided. In the relationship between parents and children, both sides must be considerate of each other. In the relationship between a husband and wife, there are certain initiatives a wife must take and certain responses that a husband must make, and vice-versa. If it is one-sided it will topple over. And if one-sided relationships do not work in human experience, what makes us think that one-sided relationships will work with respect to the structure and the function of the interaction that takes place between us and God? There is something that we must do in order to maintain a right relationship with God.

Malachi said in the first chapter of his book that "a son honors his father and a servant respects his master, but the people of God despise God." The people said, "Well, how is it that we have despised you?" And the Lord answered, "You have offered polluted bread on my altar." You have given me trash and mess and refuse and dung and garbage. You have given far less than your best. And that doesn't work with Uncle Sam. Try that for taxes or tuition or rent, or mortgage, or clothes, or the car note. All of these must consist of serious, regular, and substantial payment, and yet we think we can stroll into the presence of the Almighty and do less for God than we do for ourselves, our conveniences, and our creature comforts.

The prophet Malachi declares that we have left God; we have departed from him; we are mouthing the words *I believe,* but our actions are not consistent with what we are saying. But then the prophet comes to chapter 3, where he announces that God says to us, "If you will return to me, I will return to you." If you do something, then I will do something. And it is at this point that the prophet says, "Will a man rob God?" Will anybody be so bold and brazen as to rob the living God? Will people in their mortality and weakness and shortness and frailty and brevity of days on earth rob God, while they are open to all kinds of accidents and tragedies and contingencies and calamities and setbacks and illnesses and uncertainties? Will we in our weakness and vulnerability and dependency rob God? The God who owns and sustains the whole universe! Will we dare rob God?

The question is not whether a person will steal from God. For when you steal from somebody, that means you are taking from behind that person's back. The person from whom you steal can't see what you are doing. But when you rob somebody, you are doing it to their person, in their face. You are openly assaulting and assailing the victim. You are robbing and traumatizing a person in the person's presence. And so the question is, will a person dare rob, assault, and assail the person of God? God, all powerful, all knowing, all wise, all loving, and everywhere present! Will anybody dare be that ungrateful?

Everything we have comes from God. We brought nothing into this world, and we will take nothing out of it. There are no pockets in a shroud, no case in a casket, and no Brink's truck in a funeral processional. If you have anything, God gave it to you! I know there are those who say, "I got it on my own; I did it for myself; I worked my job; I got up every morning and went to my job." But who woke you up? Who started you on your way? Who gave you strength to stand and life to live and breath to breathe and love to enjoy and hope to hold onto? Who opened the job door up for you and gave you the opportunity to work? The writer of the book of James says, "Every good and perfect gift cometh from above, from the Father in whom there is no variableness neither shadow of turning." Jesus said, "freely you have received, freely give." And Paul said, "What have you got that you didn't receive?" When will we learn to shout like Paul: "I am what I am but by the grace of God!"

So God said to the people through Malachi, the prophet, You have robbed me. And the people said, How have we robbed you? And God said, You have done it by withholding your tithes and your offerings. And if you really want to mend your broken relationship with me, if you really want to keep faith with me, if you really want to pick up the pieces of your shattered life and put them back together again...here's how you do it: Bring ye all the tithes into the storehouse, not just a little piece of it, not just a pinch of it, but all of it. Don't hold back part of it. Pay the whole thing, the whole tenth, without robbing God, without cheating, without defrauding God. Malachi says, "Bring ye all the tithes into the storehouse."

Now the word *storehouse* is translated from the Hebrew word that means "the temple treasure." The same word is used in Nehemiah 13:12, which says all Judah brought the tithe of the coin and the new wine and the oil into the treasury. Which treasury? The United Way? Neighborhood Charities? March of Dimes? United Negro College Fund? NAACP? Black United Front? None of these!

The word means the treasuries of the house of God. The tithe is explicitly and exclusively a holy offering unto God through the institution of the congregation of the people of God—the church. This concept of the tithe is demonstrated and substantiated in Leviticus 27:30, which says the tithe is the Lord's. It is holy unto the Lord. And there is further documentation that the Hebrew word in Malachi that we translate as *storehouse* refers to the temple treasury, for 2 Chronicles 31:11 says, "Then Hezekiah commanded to prepare chambers in the house of the LORD; and they prepared them, and brought in the offerings and the tithes and the dedicated things faithfully." Thus the tithe was to be brought into the house of the Lord and to be dedicated wholly unto the Lord. Now, that much is explicit! That's not my opinion. It's in the Word. It's God's plan for the people of God.

Where shall we tithe? Not to the radio or television evangelist, because you are not going to call them when you get sick, or when you need somebody to preach a relative's funeral, or when you need somebody to come to the hospital to see you. You are not going to call Billy Graham or Oral Roberts or Robert Schuller or any of those folks. You are going to call some preacher in town. And if you are going to call on a preacher in town, you need to pay your tithe to a church in town. The church is the central agency of God on earth. And as long as we faithfully bring our tithes into the church's treasury, the church will always have sufficient resources to meet human needs, and the name of the Lord will be exalted, and the gospel will be preached, and missions will grow throughout the world.

The tithe is a basic admission that God is the source of your life. And if you shout without bringing your tithe, you are shouting on credit! "Bring ye all the tithes into the storehouse." Don't split it up, but let it make a powerful and meaningful impact upon the life of Memphis and the life of the world. Let it be a witness of life and hope. Let it be a light shining in the darkness of confusion and disruption. Let it be one place where young folks can come and be safe. Let it be one place where teenagers can come and be helped. Let it be one place where anybody can come and get a meal and help and hope and love and joy! Let it be a house of prayer for all nations! Let it be a rock in a weary land and a shelter in a time of storm!

" 'And prove me now herewith,' saith the Lord of hosts." Prove me now! Let me demonstrate that I will "open the windows of heaven and pour out blessings that there shall not be room enough to receive them." The cry of the world is that we don't have enough. We don't have enough joy! We don't have enough peace! We don't have enough hope! But when we learn to trust God, when we stop robbing God, when we learn to seek God first, we will no longer have to cry *not enough*, but we will be able to shout *not room enough*!

Lord, hasten that day! Amen.

*T*HE ECONOMIC TEST OF SPIRITUALITY

C. Roy Stauffer

*Jesus and money are bound together. This sermon is an
unashamed merger of Christian faith and money. When
people are tired of hearing about money, they are
susceptible to losing their spiritual energy.*

Proverbs 11:24–25a, 28; Matthew 6:19–21, 24

Last Sunday in my sermon I made the following statement:
"Economics lies at the center of all spiritual decision-making."
Nobody commented on that statement, even though I repeated it
at least three times in the sermon. I wonder if you heard it...and
how it struck you. Would you agree with it? Is it a fact of life in
our modern secular world that you would accept?

Not only is it true in our modern world, but it was also true
of the ancient world in which Jesus lived. One's attitude toward
money and material possessions determines one's relationship
with God. Why else would our Lord have had more to say about it
than any other single subject? More than one-third of all Jesus'
parables, and one-sixth of all the verses in the Gospels, deal with
the use of one's possessions, particularly money. Jesus had sixteen times as much to say about money as he did about baptism,
and thirty-two times as much to say about money as he did about
the Lord's supper. Since that's the case, I don't think it's wrong
for the church to emphasize stewardship of one's money once a
year, or for me to preach two or three sermons on it each year. In
fact, to anyone who might make that classic comment—"Every
time I go to church they're always talking about money"—I would
say that's more a comment on your church attendance than it is
about the church's asking for money (at least here at Lindenwood).

Roy Stauffer is senior pastor of Lindenwood Christian Church in Memphis, Tennessee.

80

Maybe that's why one particular preacher chose to do what he did. When he was being interviewed by a church to become their minister and preached a "trial sermon," all the church members thought it was great! So they called him to be their minister. The next Sunday his preaching was great—but it was the same sermon. And again and again, the same sermon. Several weeks later the elders asked to meet with him. They said they had called him to be their minister because of his great preaching. "But," they said, "why do you keep preaching the same sermon over and over again?" The minister replied, "When you've heard that one, I'll preach another one." Maybe that's the way Jesus felt about the subject of money, and why he had so much to say about it.

Jesus realized that one's relationship with God is helped or hindered by one's possessions, especially one's money. It is the most important factor affecting spiritual decision-making. It will either make or break one's relationship to God, because each of us must decide which it will be—God or mammon. If you choose God and express that decision with your giving, nothing can break your relationship with God. But if you decide that money, mammon, and materialism are more important to you, even though you might give "lip service" to God, nothing can rescue you from a spiritual vacuum and all that it brings.

There's a lot of talk today about our modern American secular culture and the fact that the more prosperous people become, the less joy they seem to find in their lives. The story is told about one man who had accumulated vast riches but remained unhappy. He went to a very wise counselor to inquire about the reason for his gloom. The wise counselor took him to a window and asked him what he saw. "I see people down on the street," he replied. "Now," said the wise counselor, "look in the mirror on the wall and tell me what you see." "I see myself," he responded. "Yes, and herein lies your problem," said the counselor. "The mirror is made of glass, and the window is made of glass; but when you add a little silver to it, you no longer see other people. You see only yourself."

Of course, in the teachings of Jesus, the rich young ruler is the epitome of the same lesson. How rich, yet how miserable. But thank goodness, there are more and more people waking up today and realizing the emptiness of our modern materialistic, consumer-mentality society today.

No wonder Jesus had more to say about money than any other subject. More than he said about prayer, for the wrong attitude toward money keeps you from prayer. More than he said about worship and faith, for those who worship mammon cannot worship God; those who trust in money will not trust in God. More than he said about even the scriptures, for those who prefer *Money* magazine, *The Wall Street Journal,* and the daily stock market report to the Bible won't have a chance at a strong spiritual life. Isn't it amazing how so many of us today who would never miss the daily stock market report or *The Wall Street Journal* or even the daily newspaper don't mind skipping their daily Bible reading? No wonder Jesus had more to say about money and the things that money can buy, and the right use of possessions, than any other subject.

I also wonder sometimes if Jesus had as hard a time getting people to listen to his teachings about the Christian use of money as most preachers do today? It's no secret that at least 20 percent of those who would normally attend church will stay away if they know the sermon's going to be on this subject. When some church members know the minister is going to talk about Christian stewardship in terms of money, pledges, and the church budget, that's the Sunday they will decide to go visit Aunt Tilda, or be too tired to go to church. So, if Jesus talked about money and stewardship more than any other subject, I wonder how many avoided hearing him. Maybe that's why Jesus said such things as, "Many are called, but few respond," or the difference between the broad way and the narrow way, and which way the multitudes will choose. Still, Jesus never backed off! He never chose just to preach popular subjects to draw a crowd but used every opportunity to instruct people in the right use of the things they possessed.

Let's look at one or two of Jesus' teachings about money and possessions and see what he had to say. I guess just about as familiar a teaching of Jesus as there is is when he says in the Sermon on the Mount: "Seek ye first the kingdom of God, and all these things shall be yours as well." He meant joy, peace, patience, kindness, courage, love, and all the other gifts of the Spirit—but he meant even more than that. The people had been worrying about money and material possessions—what they would eat, what they would wear, where they would live, and so forth. And Jesus said, "Seek ye first the kingdom of God, and all these things will be taken care of." You don't need to worry!

Some folks may not catch the connection between money and this teaching about the kingdom. But just think a moment about what money can buy compared to the joys of the kingdom, and you will then see what Jesus is saying. Money can buy recreation…but it cannot buy happiness. It can buy a bed…but it can't buy a good night's sleep. It can buy books…but it cannot buy wisdom. It can buy "friends"…but it cannot buy friendship. It can buy food…but it cannot buy an appetite. It can buy a house…but it cannot buy a home. It can buy medicine…but it cannot buy health. But, if you seek first the kingdom of God, all these other things will be yours as well.

There is also a sense of urgency in this teaching of Jesus. He says to "seek the kingdom now"—right away, before it is too late. He says this as a warning, because there comes a time when it is too late, when the opportunity is gone. If we seek other things first, ahead of the kingdom, we may suddenly discover one day that we have missed the opportunity for the kingdom. Who knows what tomorrow may bring? And nowhere is this any clearer than when Jesus tells about the rich man who decided to build bigger barns, rather than seek the kingdom. And then one day he suddenly dies, before he ever gets to enjoy those bigger barns. And in the parable, he is actually called a "fool." And what about you? What are your priorities? Where are your investments for tomorrow, not knowing what tomorrow may bring?

It all comes down to another basic and well-known teaching of Jesus, and that has to do with the choice between "God or mammon." Jesus said: "No man can serve two masters: for either he will hate the one, and love the other; or else he will hold to the one and despise the other. Ye cannot serve God and mammon"(Matthew 6:24, KJV.)

We all know this! It's no big secret to us! But the question is: "Have we accepted it?" And the honest truth of the matter is that too many of us continue to worship the things we should use, and use the things we should worship. But sooner or later, we will all discover that money is a good servant, but it is a poor master.

I love the story about an incident that happened in a very elegant home where several families had been invited to a dinner party. As everyone was mixing and mingling and enjoying themselves, there came the piercing scream of one small child. It seems he had gotten his hand stuck in a very expensive vase in this elegantly decorated home. His panicked cries caused all the adults to panic too. But try as they might, they couldn't get his stuck hand out of the vase. Finally, the host said, "We'll just have to smash the vase." When they did, and the pieces shattered in every direction, it was then that they discovered that the little boy's fist was tightly wrapped around a single penny he had seen in the bottom of the vase. And that was why he couldn't get his hand out! Is that not a parable about many of us adults too? So often we shatter the truly beautiful things of life in our overpowering love for money.

A third and final teaching of Jesus that helps us see why it is that economics lies at the center of all spiritual decision-making is his teaching about "hearts and treasures." Jesus said very simply: "Where your treasure is, there your heart will be also" (Matthew 6:21). Notice the very clear and specific order of things. Jesus didn't say, "Where your heart is, there will your treasure be also." No, he said, "Where your treasure is, there your heart will be also."

Most of us in the church get this one backwards. And so, when it comes to the annual stewardship campaign, there are always those who say, "If we just develop spirituality in the church, we won't have to ask for money—for it will come naturally." I used to believe that way myself. But now I think Jesus is saying something quite different. Jesus knew us better than we know ourselves. He knew that it's where we put our money that our real interest lies.

Last Sunday a guest teacher in one of our Sunday school classes made an interesting observation about this. He said if you don't believe it, then go out and purchase a sizable amount of stock in some company. He then said that the next morning he would guarantee that when you went out to get your newspaper, it would not be the comics or the sports page to which you would turn first. You might quickly glance at the headlines, but the first place you would turn in the newspaper would be the stock market report to see how your stock was doing. Where your treasure is, there will your heart be also!

Another minister tells of the experience he had in his church with a member who used to be one of those "CME" members— you know, those are the ones who only come on Christmas, Mother's Day and Easter. But when their church entered into a major fund-raising campaign, this man gave more than a tenth of the total amount they were trying to raise. Even more amazing than that, the next Sunday the man was in church...and the next... and the next. He wanted to check on his investment. And within four years he was chairman of the board!

Jesus was so right. Where you put your money, that is where your interest is. It has been said that in any church—Lindenwood included—if you had a list of how much money each member made a year, and how much of that they gave to the church, you could quickly make a list of which members would be in church most Sundays. The man who makes $100,000 a year but gives only $1,000 or so, cannot be counted on when the chips are down. But the woman living on Social Security who gives $500 a year can truly be counted on. Those who give seriously to Christ and His church are the ones most interested in the kingdom of God, and the ones Christ can count on.

Yes, economics lies at the center of all spiritual decision-making. That's because the way we choose to use our money reveals the state of our souls...and our relationship to God.

$\mathcal{T}$HE DAY DAD PAYS THE BILLS

Eugene W. Brice

> *"Money" is the word. The sermon is most helpful in*
> *clarifying what money is good for. This sermon helps*
> *people discover how they use it or if it uses them.*
> *Concrete, practical, and revelatory!*

Luke 6:37–38

Everyone walks on tiptoes the day Dad pays the bills. Does it happen like this at *your* house? There they are—those envelopes with little windows in them, all stacked up, and there he is, brow furrowed, face anxious, checkbook out and active. And there's a bit of tension in the air as the little monthly drama is played out, with many undercurrents of hidden meaning behind it all.

There is Dad, worried that no matter what he makes, it's always used up in this monthly ritual, wondering what they would do if a *real* emergency came up, feeling inadequate because he's not making more money. There is Mom, angry because her efforts to cut back aren't appreciated, guilty because maybe she *could* be a better manager, frustrated because she doesn't know what she can do about it all. And there is Junior, not sure *what* is going on, but wise enough to keep out of sight and shrewd enough not to ask for a new stereo on this particular day. Or maybe, at your house, you can change the assignments, and it is the day *Mom* pays the bills.

Survey after survey shows it—there are more family arguments about money than about any other subject. The three

Eugene Brice has recently retired from serving University Christian Church in Fort Worth, Texas, as its senior minister. His most recent volume of sermons is entitled *The Illusion of Excellence* (Chalice Press).

runners-up, in order, are children, sex, and in-laws, but money keeps leading the band year after year. Good health in the family, then, depends on an understanding of the role of money in our lives. This is made somewhat more difficult because money plays more than one role in life. Consider, for example:

I. *For many of us, money is a deceiver*, a Pied Piper playing a tune seeking to convince us that it is the answer to the problems of life. If we just had a little more, life would be fine. It should not take more than a look about us to show us that that's wrong. Compared to the rest of the world, *we have a little more*, right now, all of us do, even the most desperate ones among us.

I thought of this last week, in a short ten-minute span of watching TV. There was first a short feature on how to cook leftovers, how most Americans, especially children, hate to eat leftovers. So the feature told how to make that old leftover roast beef attractive enough so your children would eat it. Then immediately, there was a commercial for a gourmet cat food, showing the lovely Persian cat eating out of a crystal serving dish. And immediately, then, the newscast which followed showed the empty-eyed people of Somalia lying in rows on the parched ground, waiting for death, with nothing to eat, *nothing*.

Money is a deceiver, in that it permits us to look only one way when evaluating our present state. Jesus' parable is the classic statement of it. A man with property, ripe fields, full barns, but who was not content. He saw only riper fields and fuller barns, and his life leaked away in his pursuit of that deceiver, money.

In our consumer society, almost everything we see and read and hear reinforces that deception. There are things that will bring you happiness if you just buy them. No wonder there is frustration and anger among the poorer people of our land! Television shows them what they do not have that many do. They hear pitches about $40,000 cars and $500 cameras and $50 shirts, but their most immediate problem is what to have for supper. Again, most of us don't think of these folk when considering what we have. If we only had *more* money, we think, things would be fine.

If that were the case, it ought to follow that the more money a family has, the fewer arguments about money it would have, right? *Wrong*! Among the affluent in our society, with salaries over $100,000 annually, money still leads the list as the most frequent cause of controversy in the family. Indeed, and strangely, studies show that salary increases lead to far more fights at home than salary cuts.

Money is a deceiver, dangling always in front of us an elusive rainbow of enough—which never comes. There are always more Joneses for us to keep up with, once we've overtaken some of them. I've always liked the story that appeared about ten years ago of the fellow named Bob who wasn't as successful as his friend Joe and was extremely jealous. It especially provoked him that Joe often called him on the phone from Joe's car. That always ruined Bob's day—he didn't have anything, but Joe had a phone in his car. So Bob vowed to get a phone in *his* car, too. He borrowed some money and had a phone installed in his car, and immediately put in a call to Joe's mobile number. "Joe," Bob said, "are you in your car?" "Sure," Joe said. "Well listen," said Bob, "guess where I'm calling you from." Joe paused and then said, "Bob, would you hold on just a minute? My other phone is ringing." Almost to illustrate our point, that story doesn't have quite the ring it had when it appeared ten years ago because phones in cars have become so much more common. It takes running fast to keep up.

Always beyond our reach, this rainbow, always a valley away. Money plays the role of deceiver as it seeks to convince us in our families that if we just had more, life would be okay.

II. But there is a better role that money plays. *Money is a servant*. By itself, it is worth nothing. If you were starving to death, a million dollars on a desk before you would do nothing by itself. If you were freezing to death, you could burn it and get a bit of warmth. But money is of real value only when it is used. Money is a wonderful servant, but a terrible master.

There are homes where money is the master, requiring us to do things for it that amaze us. If money wants us to fight with one another at home, we'll do that. It will ask us to lie, and we'll do that. It will ask us to cheat, and we'll do that. It will sometimes ask us to abandon our church, and we'll even do that if money is involved. It is a harsh master, indeed, moving us here and yonder at will.

Years ago, John Wesley urged his English followers to adopt the 80-10-10 system of family finances. Figure what 80 percent of your income is, he said, and then spend it gladly. Budget yourself and enjoy spending that 80 percent. Put 10 percent of it in savings. It's yours, but you'll defer its use. And give 10 percent of it away— give it gladly and freely, pick your recipients well, and enjoy giving it. In short, he is saying, make your money your servant, and not vice versa.

III. There is a third role money plays in our lives. *Money is a creator of values.* The way we use money inevitably creates a system of values in ourselves and in our children. A woman reported once a tactless remark a friend made as the graveside service for the woman's father was completed. As they walked back to the car, the friend asked bluntly, "What did he leave you?" It shocked the woman into answering that question for herself. Although her father had not left her much in material things, he had left her a set of values and a collection of memories she would never lose.

Go back to Jesus' parable of the rich fool, and imagine a few days after the man's death the reading of his will. What did he leave his children? He left them big barns and an appetite for bigger ones. Other than that, some of *us* don't leave our children very much. The way we use our money determines what sort of values we leave those children.

An issue of *Psychology Today* contained a remarkable article to prove this. Some months before, the magazine did a reader survey on ethics and morals, seeking to determine just how ethical the American people are, and what factors enter into our morality. If the reader slightly scratched someone's car and no one saw, for example, would the reader drive away without further attention to it? Would the reader ever take sick leave when she wasn't sick? Would he take liberties on his income tax return? Would she cheat on her spouse?

Some 24,000 people filled out and returned the lengthy questionnaire. Somewhat to the surprise of the editors, the survey found that religious commitment was the second most important factor in identifying persons with high ethical standards. *Psychology Today* is not noted for any bias toward religion, and the editors admit being surprised at this finding. Their assumption, they said, was that "there are far more sinners sitting in churches than at home minding their own business." But the survey showed that people sitting in churches *do* tend to be consistently more ethical than the average person. Religious commitment was the second most important factor in identifying high ethical standards.

What came in first? What was the most accurate predictor of ethical behavior? Again, the editors were surprised. *"Only the amount given to charity was a better predictor of how closely each person's behavior corresponded to his beliefs."* That finding tested out among 24,000 readers, and many find it startling! A person's use of money, his or her willingness to give it generously, is the best predictor of that person's ethical behavior in other situations. The more tightly people hold to their money, the less likely they are to make decent and honorable decisions in the scores of little ethical dilemmas we find ourselves in daily.

This is a finding that is surprising to secular people today, and even to many church people, this statistical correlation between giving and ethical behavior. But the Bible has been saying it all along! Find a person who is unwilling to give, one who can always find a reason *not* to give, and you will find one who will be less likely to do the honorable thing about daily ethical decisions ranging in importance from cutting in line at the grocery store to marital infidelity. Values in general are taught and reflected by our use of money.

Then let me summarize it. Money can be a *deceiver*, leading you to think that its acquisition will bring you happiness. Money can be a *servant*, bringing your family order and satisfaction. Money's proper use can be the best *creator of values* your family has, and that's why we ought to bring our children into the process when we fill out our pledge card and when we pay monthly bills. They need to know how much things cost— from the monthly mortgage to the electricity bill—and they need to know and see how much the family gives to the church and other charitable institutions. It is hard to overemphasize the high potential of this moment for creating values. It can be one of the most healthy, life-molding experiences for the whole family—the day Dad pays the bills.

Let us pray: Eternal Father, even as we thank you for great material gifts, we ask you to help us use them wisely, and well, in Jesus' name. Amen.

$\mathcal{P}$ARTNERS TO THE END

R. Scott Colglazier

This sermon is creative in making the Bible story real in the church today. It speaks with clarity and passion about the whole life of the church—past, present, and future—and challenges a generation disillusioned with institutions to consider the importance of the ministry of the church in their lives and in their world.

Philippians 1:3–14

Pounding away in the chest of the apostle Paul was the heart of a preacher. A preacher! A man who longed to stand before people and proclaim the good news of Jesus Christ, a message that brings hope and light into the dark lives of people. He was willing to travel the most dangerous road, willing to risk his very own life just to preach the message, willing to endure hardship for the sake of preaching the gospel of God's grace.

However, Paul needed a partner in ministry, a congregation of people who were willing to support him with financial gifts, with their prayers, with their emotional energy. The congregation of Philippian Christians looked at this missionary of Christ—a man who dreamed of a day when every man, woman, and child would believe the gospel—and said, "As long as you travel and preach, we will support you."

It was a great deal! A partnership made in heaven for heaven's sake!

The partnership went well until one night, in a Philippian church board meeting, the outreach committee had to report sheepishly that their star minister and missionary had been thrown into jail. You can imagine the scene. A board member,

Scott Colglazier is senior minister of University Christian Church in Fort Worth, Texas. He is the author of *Finding a Faith That Makes Sense* (Chalice Press).

half asleep, jerks his head up and asks, "Now what did you say happened to him?" Another member pipes up, "I told you from the beginning that you couldn't trust him." By now the outreach chairperson is blushing a fire-engine red. (You may have to report a variety of things to the board, but no one wants to report that the preacher has just been thrown into jail.) The reporter tries to explain that details are sketchy and the charges are uncertain, but it is true that Paul's preaching tour has stopped with the slam of a jail-cell door. It's funny how everyone on the board fidgets at the same time; funny how quiet some board meetings can become.

The silence of the boardroom is broken when someone from the corner raises a hand and says, "I move that we stop all support." "I second it," someone pipes up. The chairman of the board looks at the bewildered people and asks, "Is there any discussion?"

Is there? The question which every church must answer is: Will we support the ministry? Not Scott's ministry or Becky's or Sue's or any group of professional clergy. But will we support the ministry that belongs to God, a ministry that is ultimately for the sake of the world, a ministry of love that God has given the church to complete?

The world needs the ministry of the church—that fact seems rather obvious. Millions of people are starving; military powers threaten the globe; terrorism dots the countries of the planet; drugs and alcohol ruin people's lives; personal relationships crumble; AIDS ravages bodies; death lays bare families and friends. The question is not: Does the world *need* the ministry of Christ?

The church needs the ministry—that fact seems equally obvious. Broken Christians need mending; questions of faith need intelligent answers; problems of spiritual depth need to be solved; hodgepodge theology confuses and leaves people despairing when moments of crisis come crashing down. The question is not: Does the church *need* the ministry of Christ?

The question that restlessly wiggles in our consciences this morning is: Will we *support* the ministry of the church and of Jesus Christ?

In his opening paragraph Paul encourages the church to think of their support of the ministry from three different perspectives: past, present, and future. This is why he begins his letter to the Philippians by *remembering* their past. He remembers who they are, what they have been through together; he remembers what they have done together for God's kingdom. Most of all, he remembers their partnership in the gospel. It is crucial that the church remember together. H. Richard Niebuhr spoke of the church remembering together as nothing less than an act of revelation.

What do you remember today about the church? Do you remember your first time here? Do you remember the time of your confession, your baptism, your acceptance into membership? Maybe you remember the first Sunday in this building? Maybe you could go into my study and look at the Elders Memorial Board, remembering the people behind the names. Do you remember times at a circle meeting, a pitch-in, a youth event? And do you remember the dreams and hopes? Visions of a thriving church, a full church, a serving church where God's word and God's world would be taken with the utmost seriousness and joy?

We are a people of memories; some are memories of grief and happiness, others of success and failure, but these memories beckon us to decide. You may not see anybody in the balconies this morning, but they are filled to overflowing with people who in times past gave of their time, their talent, their money. They are looking at us from the gallery and are asking: Will we support the ministry of the church?

Not only does Paul talk about the past; he also talks about the present. He speaks about his feelings of affection for the Philippians, the joy which they bring to his heart. He talks about his loyalty to them, the kindred feeling and commitments which bind them together.

What do you feel about the present? Look around. No one in this sanctuary is perfect, but there are some pretty special people here. There are people who are your friends. When you are sick, chances are somebody in this sanctuary visits you. When you go through a divorce, someone here offers care and sympathy. When you have questions about God, there is a youth group, a Sunday school class, a Monday Bible study that takes your questions seriously. Folks, I know that there have been mistakes in the past, and there will be mistakes in the future, but when it is all said and done, which of course is the only time that really matters, this is a good place to be today! For today, you can find in this sanctuary what many people look a lifetime for. I think the title of William Willimon's book is suggestive: *What's Right With the Church?* If we will open our eyes, there is a profound rightness in the present experience of church, and that profundity causes us to ask: Will we support the ministry of the church?

And of course, Paul also looks to the future with his prayers and hopes. Here is a man in prison being guarded by Roman soldiers, yet he believes in the future of the church. He looks forward to the spiritual growth of the Philippians, hoping that they will love with greater perception, intelligence, and understanding. He looks forward to that great day, that day when they will face the ultimate of ultimates, the day of Christ, when they will be filled with the fruit of righteousness.

What kind of future do you see today? There is a lot of work to be done. What hopes burn in your heart—more people in worship? Better programs? More children? Greater spiritual depth? What kind of church are we building for the future? Will there be a church for the children, a world, a place to belong as they search for meaning? Ultimately, what kind of future do we have? Will the ministry that takes place here every day make an ultimate difference on that day, the day of days when we will bow before the glorious Christ?

The tomorrows of the church demand investments today. For some of us, it is very difficult to invest ourselves in the institutional ministry of the church. Those of an older generation know well the value of institutions like family, government, church, school, service clubs. But those of us of a younger generation really don't know what to do with institutions. My first introduction to institutions came through the television news—I saw American bombs being dropped on Cambodia; I saw Kent State College students weep over shots fired by the National Guard; I saw police hosing down African-Americans as they walked through the streets; I saw beads of sweat drip off the trembling lips of a President as he resigned from office. Many of us in a younger generation have little confidence in institutional life, so we turned our resources in upon ourselves, the private concerns of family. We think nothing of buying designer clothes for kids, a large screen TV for the den, a home computer for storing the budget, an educational trip to Epcot Center, season tickets for entertainment. But to make an intense commitment to the ministry of the church, a commitment of time, skills, energy, and money, is difficult for many of us to do.

But today we are talking about the future. We are talking about the future of this church, a church that I hope will continue the helping, healing, mending ministry of Jesus Christ. Does that future rest in you? Is there any hope, any dream that could so ignite your heart that you could answer the question: Will we support the ministry of the church?

This is our stewardship season, that time of year when the challenges of next year must be met with the financial pledges of today. But we do not talk about stewardship in a vacuum. The ministry of the church is the matrix of our past, our present, and our future. All three dimensions must make a difference in how much we increase our pledge for next year.

Ernest Hemingway, who I doubt ever preached a stewardship sermon, but who did know something of money, said, "Money is important—with it you can support those things that are more important than money." How true. The ministry of Christ is worth more than all the money in the world, but without money, the ministry of Christ is muted.

I remember as a youngster watching a National Geographic special on monkeys. Scientists came up with an ingenious way to catch monkeys. They would cut out an opening in a coconut, fill it with rice, and put it in a tree. The monkey would come, slip its hand in, and grab the rice, making a fist. When the monkey made a fist, however, it couldn't get its hand out of the coconut, because the monkey would not let go of the rice. The coconut slowed the monkey down enough so that scientists could catch it.

Even when we know we should, it's hard to undo our fists and let go of our possessions and financial blessings. Friends, our moment has come to stop monkeying around! It is time to open up our hearts, minds, schedules, and checkbooks. It is time to pull together the past, present, and future, and support the ministry which is God's and which is ours, a ministry that we have as partners to the end.

BREAD, BLOOD, AND MONEY

Joseph R. Jeter, Jr.

Would you take money from the devil and use it for the service of Christ? According to this sermon, "it depends." The struggle between God and Caesar, sacred and secular, is difficult at best, but it is necessary for the human creature. This sermon calls us to the table of our Lord to share the struggle.

1 Samuel 21:1–6; Acts 10:9–16

During the three years ending with 1907, the Foreign Christian Missionary Society of the Disciples of Christ received some $25,000 in gifts from Mr. John D. Rockefeller. That sounds good, except for one thing: There were a number of people who roundly despised Mr. Rockefeller and his methods, calling him and them ruthless and monopolistic. Led by T. W. Phillips, a Pennsylvania oil man who had felt the sting of Mr. Rockefeller's operation, and by the increasingly conservative *Christian Standard*, an attempt was made to force the Society to return this "tainted" money. On the other side were those like A. McLean and even the venerable brother John W. McGarvey, who said, "I would take money from the devil and use it in the service of Christ." The controversy came to a head at the Norfolk convention that year when Mr. Phillips proposed returning the money and was soundly defeated. The money was kept; the harmony of the church was lost.

From the Rockefeller money of the nineteen-aughts to the divestment question of the late nineteen-eighties, from the support of open-membership missionaries in China to the World Council fund to combat racism in Africa, the questions of where

Joey Jeter is Granville and Erline Walker Associate Professor of Homiletics at Texas Christian University in Fort Worth, Texas. His most recent book is *Re/Membering: Meditations and Sermons for the Table of Jesus Christ* (Chalice Press).

the church's money comes from and where it goes have never been far from the center of discussion. And they have affected the overall stewardship and mission of the church. After all the personality conflicts have been boiled away, the issue often reduces to sacred vs. secular, sometimes to church vs. state. Can—should—the sacred serve the secular? Can—should—the secular serve the sacred? Does Athens have anything to do with Jerusalem, or even Indianapolis? Would *you* take money from the devil and use it in the service of Christ?

Those who argue for strict separation between the realms generally point to the words attributed to Jesus in Mark 12 and elsewhere: "Render to Caesar the things that are Caesar's, and to God the things that are God's" (v. 17, KJV). But that doesn't quite solve it, for the questions remain: What is Caesar's? What is God's? Our colleague Rita Nakashima Brock answers those questions this way:

> Caesar's image is on the coin because he symbolizes for the community of Jesus the most destructive power on earth. Like the governments of South Africa and Chile, Rome killed people who stood in its way. They even killed Jesus and others like him. The courage to choose between Caesar and God means to render to Caesar absolutely nothing, for our whole heart belongs to the God of Love. Caesar is the power that seeks to control, dominate and kill—power that enslaves human beings under legal, social and economic systems, grinding down the poor, hungry, outcast and weak. And those committed to the God of Love have no business paying allegiance to power like that. (*Impact* 19:43)

Whatever you think of that argument, it does vitiate a too-easy separation of realms. Church and state, sacred and secular, are "mushed" together in our world, and our determination to serve God in that mush is fraught with great difficulty. As I see it, the biblical drama is also played out in that mush. The two texts I have chosen to examine seem, at least at first glance, to be moving in opposite directions.

In the twenty-first chapter of 1 Samuel, David is on the run from Saul, who seeks to kill him. He comes to the priestly center at Nob and asks Ahimelech the priest for bread. David is hungry. The priest, however, has no common bread, only sacred bread, the Bread of the Presence, kept on the altar before YHWH. David is desperate and deceives the priest, telling him that he is on an important mission for the king. The priest wavers but tells David that only the ritually pure may eat of the bread. David assures the priest that he and "the men he has waiting for him" have maintained sexual continence on the mission. The priest yields and gives the bread to David. Later on, Ahimelech and all the priests at Nob save one are murdered by Saul for their complicity with David, but that's another sermon, as is the fact that the bread was obtained by duplicitous means, as is the fact that the remarks about women are stereotypical and offensive. What I ask you to engage in this text is that sacred substance, in this case the Bread of the Presence, was used for secular purposes: the feeding, as the priest thought, of soldiers—in actuality, of a fugitive. And the only concern seemed to be that some attention be given to ritual purity, or at least that ritual purity not be totally ignored.

Our second text is more familiar, a scene from the Cornelius story in Acts 10. Peter is praying on the roof when he sees a vision of all kinds of animals being lowered on a sheet from heaven. A voice tells him to "kill and eat," but Peter shows his loyalty to the sacred dietary laws and refuses. Three times the voice commands him to eat, and three times he refuses. The vision then leaves, and Peter is left very perplexed and confused. The scene is pivotal. Whether or not it was originally intended to broaden the mission of Jesus' followers beyond the Jews to the Gentiles, it certainly served that purpose. And Peter's confusion at the moment is certainly understandable in light of the momentous words the voice spoke: "What God has called ritually pure, you shall not call impure." It is easy for us to agree with this divine voice; it was not so easy for Peter. William Willimon puts it this way:

> [These ritual laws] identified faithfulness in the midst
> of incredible pressure to forsake the faith, drop one's
> particularities and become a good citizen of the Em-
> pire. A little pork here, a pinch of incense to Caesar
> there, and it will not be long before the faith commu-
> nity will be politely obliterated. We must not read
> this story from the safe vantage point of a majority
> religion where broadmindedness and toleration cost
> the majority nothing, but rather, read the story as it
> was first heard—from the minority point of view,
> people for whom a bit of pork or a pinch of incense or
> a little intermarriage was a matter of life and death
> for the community.[1]

What we have in this text is the exact opposite of the first one. In 1 Samuel the sacred is put to secular use; in this text the secular intrudes upon the sacred. In both cases the distinctions between sacred and secular are blurred. And perhaps greater still is the problem that, when the pure comes in contact with/encounters/collides with the impure, we tend not to think that the impure has become more pure (which it may well have), but rather that the pure has become compromised, adulterated, impure. A hundred years ago, Jacob Creath, Jr., a prominent Disciples preacher, fought against such innovations as the organ and missionary societies by saying that "if we make one slipgap in the fathers Campbell, all of Romanism will come rushing in, and we will be no more" (paraphrased from memory).

Creath would not have been happy with these texts, nor would anyone seeking clarity about where the church's money should come from and where it should go. The upshot, at least as I see it, is that the Bible does not let us off the hook on this one. The burden of decision, of faithful response, is not removed. The biblical answer to the question, "Would you take money from the devil and use it in the service of Christ?" appears to be: "That depends"—because in both of our texts, while the question of ritual purity is bent, it is not absent. In the David-Ahimelech story the question of what is right colors the entire story, and the deception and violence that drag the characters down are drawn against standards of conduct that are to be kept. In the *Acts* account, ritual purity is not set aside or ignored; it is rather *expanded* to include a broader community of animals (and people) than Peter had ever dreamed. Perhaps the best cognate for ritual purity in our situation is covenant righteousness. And, if both of these terms put you off, substitute simply "remember who you are." Since the demarcation between sacred and secular is not clear and apparently never has been, the clear and persistent call to us is to stand firm in our allegiance to God and affirm that covenant of righteousness that exists between God and God's people. So, when the two worlds collide—stop, think, remember who you are, remember the covenant into which you were baptized, and then act accordingly.

Some years ago I heard T. J. Liggett, for whom my respect is boundless, reflect upon a board meeting at Christian Theological Seminary. At the meeting the trustees approved a major financial campaign, after which T. J. surprised them by introducing a new program which was to run concurrently, a program for reaching out to people in what was then called the Third World. The trustees were aghast. They told him that the idea was good, but the timing was terrible. Why did he want to do this at the same time they were questing for money? "Because," he said, "our immortal souls are at stake." He went on to say something like: "We can only get money from those who have it, but we must not lose our souls or the soul of our institution in the process."

I speak to you this morning as one who feeds my family on the gifts of others—some of whom I know, most of whom I don't; I clothe my family because dedicated people like Gilbert Davis and Bob Gartman went out looking for those gifts; and I have no doubt that I shelter my family through some gifts that represent ill-gotten money, money gotten at the expense and oppression of the poor. The money you seek and I spend is, like us, pure and impure, sacred and secular. Would you give the Bread of the Presence to soldiers? Or perhaps more to the point, would you give money committed to the kingdom of God to revolutionary groups in Africa? Would you eat food which every fiber of your being tells you is an abomination? Or perhaps more to the point, would you invest in companies doing business in South Africa? Would you allow the military to recruit on seminary campuses? Would you take money from the devil and use it in the service of Christ? Or would you take money from Christ and use it to try to save the devil?

There are no easy answers to these questions. Well, there are, but they aren't much good. However, while we are not let blithely off the hook, we are graced with repeated biblical admonitions to take ritual purity, or covenant righteousness, seriously. While our decisions are not made for us, we are encouraged to make those decisions in light of the gospel, because the immortal souls of those who do development work, those who enjoy the fruit of that work, and the institutions we serve and love, really are at stake. Therefore, sometimes our answer must be *yes,* and sometimes it must be *no.*

I want to leave you with one little suggestion about a place where we might begin to take this matter seriously. As Disciples, when we hear texts that seem to revolve around the substances of bread and blood, we naturally think of that moment in our worship where bread and wine, body and blood, manifest the presence of Christ to us at the table. And while that's critically important, I think that these texts may be leading us in a slightly different direction. I suggest that the place in our worship where the line between sacred and secular gets most blurry and the terrain most soft is at the moment, after the deacons have brought the offering forward during the singing of the doxology, when the elder or minister holds the plate in her or his hands and offers prayer. Under the aegis of these texts, I see that as a crucial moment: the secular becomes sacralized, the sacred expands to embrace the secular. And I further suggest that this moment has become the most banal and insipid part of our whole liturgy. I have been going to church for eons, and I cannot remember a single prayer at this moment of our worship that was more than mumbled mush. Whether it's a farmer elder in a pastorless rural church praying over twelve crumpled dollars in a cracked wooden plate or a group of church bureaucrats holding up for photographers an oversized one million dollar check representing a corporate donation, that is a moment of powerful potential and great danger for the church.

So I would like to commission one of you or a group of you—nobody could do this but you, I think—to write for us some prayers and reflections: prayers for various seasons and occasions that would take this moment seriously, that would lift up the covenant righteousness that is embedded in and demanded of this moment, and that would track and reflect upon the two vectors of this moment—where the money comes from and where it goes. Such would not only aid our work in stewardship and development; it could revitalize a dreary part of our worship and lead us toward new reflection and new attitudes about the task we have before us.

Whenever anybody does the same thing over and over and over, it tends to lose its savor. Should that happen to you, it might be helpful to remember the heritage in which you stand, to remember that your ministry is broader and deeper than others might know—not punching numbers into a calculator, but saving souls. I wanted to tell you that and to tell you walkers of the blurred line, you pilgrims through this mushy land, that I love and respect you, that I'm grateful for your ministry and for my ministry that you make possible. Our allegiance is to the God of Love. Let all we do be to God's glory, now and forever. Amen.

---

[1] William Willimon, *Acts* (Louisville: Westminster John Knox Press, 1988), p. 96.

SINS OF COMMISSION, OMISSION, AND NO MISSION

Donald L. Lanier

> *The people of God have always fallen under judgment*
> *when they confuse themselves with their mission. This*
> *sermon is a powerful and fresh reminder of the relation-*
> *ship between mission and spiritual vitality. Unless we*
> *serve a living God, we will die.*

The headline screamed at me as I turned the page in the paper: "Sins of Commission, Omission, and No Mission." A Lutheran pastor[1] was making the point that, as Christians, we ordinarily identify sins in one of two categories: commission and omission. But there's another variety: the sins of *no* mission. That's the state of aimlessness that infects so many in the pew and the pulpit. It is the tendency just to get through one more meeting, or one more year without upsetting someone, or having one more squabble about abortion, homosexuality, or Basic Mission Finance. It is the sin of just getting by.

The 1980s were dubbed the Decade of Greed, highlighted with the emergence of Yuppies, Rolex watches, Reeboks, Michael Milken, Charles Keating, and Donald Trump. The 1990s may be the Decade of Retreat. "Downsizing" is a more politically correct way to say it, but retreat is what it is.

It is pulling back, cutting back, reducing our corporate ministries because the funds are not there. In some cases, perhaps, pruning is a better metaphor, because pruning has a therapeutic function that allows for more growth elsewhere.

But by-and-large, the church is in retreat. It is a *forced* retreat; we are not doing it willingly. It is being done with heavy hearts, because the vision is gone. To an increasing number of people, it no longer seems important to bring hope and life to

---

Donald L. Lanier is senior pastor of Harvard Avenue Christian Church in Tulsa, Oklahoma.

the dispossessed in faraway places. The needs closer to home are more interesting. A new isolationism is growing; our circle of compassion is shrinking, and it is not likely to stop even at the local community. If the sin of no mission is truly among us, our vision will keep shrinking until, eventually, "I" will be the only one I really care about.

Let sociologists explain *why* this is happening. We who love the church and believe in its mission must decide what to *do*. We could appoint study committees and research groups, but that is a major part of the problem. We usually invite people to meet and *discuss* mission; we seldom invite them to *do* mission. We spend much time and energy meeting, preparing, planning, studying, strategizing and reviewing, but little time and energy actually *doing* the mission of Jesus Christ.

My next-door neighbor, a dentist, left his practice for a week last summer to go with other dentists to Central America on a medical mission, sponsored by his congregation. They do it every year! A surgeon I know is part of a special project in the Presbyterian Church that encourages physicians to take a month to help in an overseas medical facility.

The way to capture the vision of mission is to *do* mission. Charles Bayer, in an important book called *A Guide to Liberation Theology for Middle-Class Congregations,* writes, "In some arenas we already know it is easier to act our way into a new set of feelings—or beliefs—than to think our way into a new set of actions" (p. 131).

Praxis holds the key to recovery of mission vision in the Christian Church (Disciples of Christ). It is a three-step process: (1) preparation, including study, prayer, and dialogue with those in need about *what* is needed; (2) action; and (3) reflection.

To plunge into a project without proper preparation is a prescription for failure. Reflection is also critical in order to ask: "What does this mean?"[2]

Our senior-high youth spent a week one summer working at a Habitat for Humanity project in Tijuana, Mexico. Before they left, they listened to others who had been on work trips. They also learned about Habitat for Humanity. Their sponsors tried to prepare our upper-middle-class youth for the poverty they were about to see. But no one can do that adequately. They had to *experience* it to believe it.

When they returned, they did not report to the congregation for nearly three months. They wanted time to reflect on what they had done and what it meant. Out of that process, they decided to work one Saturday a month with Habitat projects here in Tulsa. The youth are now among our strongest supporters of outreach.

Studies show that, increasingly, people are relying on their own experiences to authenticate what they believe. There may have been a time when people depended on a trusted political figure, the pastor, or some other authority figure for guidance. But today, they are trusting their experiences. If it happens to *them*, they can believe it. If they see with their own eyes, hold it in their hands, smell it or taste it—it's *real*.

Praxis, then, is the key for mission renewal: preparation, action, and reflection. It is a cycle that spins off other projects, because once people taste the thrill of actually *doing* something of value, they can't be stopped.

It doesn't have to be an overseas project. It can begin in your community. Any social agency would welcome the infusion of Christians looking for hands-on experience.

It also can start within your congregation. Stop calling your committees *committees*. Call them missions. Ask your church school teachers how teaching fulfills the mission of Christ. Are they not doing important work in the name of God? Ask your evangelism callers to think about their *mission*. Are they not carrying God's love when they visit prospective members? Isn't there a mission of hospitality in welcoming the stranger among us?

Even the property department is a mission. One year a debate arose as we were building the budget and trying to stretch our pledged income around all of the expenses. Several in that meeting suggested that part of the property budget should be considered outreach, because our building is used by many community groups. We provide a place to meet and include utilities and custodial service without cost to many such groups. Isn't that an expression of the church's mission?

If we think in terms of mission and ministry rather than committees and departments, our faith might be revolutionized!

The church will regain its vitality only as it becomes involved in *doing* the work of ministry. A church that is concerned about its low rate of baptism, its lagging growth rate and its budget crisis needs a mission program. Such a church has forgotten what it is. It is not the Sunday morning social club. It is not the weekly reunion of Shy Persons Anonymous.

The church is the living body of Christ, not the petrified remains of an ancient Hebrew. The difference between the living and the dead is that the living *move*. *They do things*.

If our congregations are to breathe life again, it will be because we have discovered *why* we are the church. We are the church in order to make things happen, to make a difference, and to make the presence of God real in the midst of the world's chaos.

There are quiet times, to be sure, when the church is gathered to be infused with a new birth of God's Spirit. There are funny times and tender times when we celebrate God's gift of love that is so rich among us. But God forbid that we lose sight of *why* we are so blessed. We are blessed in order to become a blessing. We are guilty of gluttony if we gorge ourselves on the rich fellowship of Christians and go not out to share the feast. Yea, verily, we shall die from over-eating.

---

[1] Gerald Seaman, "Mission in Action," *Lutheran Life,* Sept. 1993, p. 14.

[2] *Preparation* ought to include a dialogue, if possible, with those who are to be helped. More likely, it would be with those who are already working in the area. Our preparation must include *their* assessment of the need. *Reflection* is just as critical, because it helps assess the significance of what was done. Each participant needs to assimilate experience, emotion, and meaning. "Did we *really* help?" "Did we build 'community' with each other, and with those whom we were trying to help?" "Do we understand the root causes of poverty any better now?" "Were we able to express God's love in what we did?"

Bruce Van Voorhis, a missionary to Hong Kong, recently said: "Our faith is based on love, and mission is love in action. Love is at the heart of our faith; mission is the reflection of our love (and God's love)...To do mission is not an option of our faith, it is the witness of our faith."

STEWARDSHIP–HORIZONTAL LIVING

Kim Gage Ryan

This sermon helps the preacher move toward a more invitational understanding of stewardship and life. The preacher's positive approach to giving as the opening of the heart to the wider world and the opening of the soul to God encourages hearers to open themselves to the joy of giving by seeing the joy of life that is possible through this act.

Psalm 37

This is the third week for us in a three-week series concerning stewardship. I don't know what I was thinking when I chose to be the third preacher to give a sermon about stewardship. Rick and Jay have already said it all, haven't they? They said all the good stuff. Rick (Frost) preached two weeks ago, challenging us with the question: "Is our giving worthy of who we are?" and Jay (Self) offered that beautiful analogy of stewardship as what roots us like a tree, or else we may find ourselves more like tumbleweeds. Whenever I thought about stewardship ideas this week I had to admit, "Been there...done that."

One thing I held on to, however, was a good joke. I overheard someone tell it to Rick two weeks ago, and I made him promise not to tell Jay. I wrote it down so I'd be sure to get it right, and here it is: A little boy was in church and it came time for the offering. His father gave him a dollar to put in the offering plate. The plate came down the pew. Dad nodded for him to put his dollar in; the little boy shook his head and held on tightly. Dad nodded; little boy held on tightly. Finally the plate went on without his dollar. All through the service the child held on tightly to the dollar. When the service was over and they were leaving, the minister reached out his hand to shake hands and the little boy put the dollar in the minister's

Kim Gage Ryan is associate pastor of Broadway Christian Church in Columbia, Missouri.

hand. The minister was surprised, "Why, thank you, but why are you giving me this dollar?" "I'm giving it to you," the child responded, "because my dad says you are the poorest preacher he's ever known."

That little boy reminds me of another little boy, three years old, in worship for one of his first times. His grandpa was visiting. It came time for the offering. Grandpa took out his wallet and gave a dollar to his grandson. The boy's eyes lit up. The offering plates were on their way, came down the aisle, down the pew. In this true story, the grandpa reached over, took the dollar out of the child's hand, put it in the plate, and sent it on its way. In that moment the child's horizons were immediately widened. In that moment that child received a new understanding about what it means to be in worship and to participate, and that child did *not* like it one little bit. In that one moment that child went from delight to dismay. His eyes opened wide, his mouth opened wide, and the sound of a cry, "NO!" was just beginning. Well, you have never seen a grandpa move so fast—out came the wallet, out came the dollar, into the hand before any sound could be produced, and just in time. The mouth closed, the eyes brightened, and the service went on uninterrupted.

Now that little boy reminds me of...myself! Being asked to give when I'm not quite sure I want to do that. It feels good to hold that dollar in my hand. All too soon it seems like it's taken out of my hand and sent on its way. My inclination is to hold on to it tightly in my clinched fist.

Yet Christians are offered an entirely different approach by which to navigate our lives, an alternative to tight-fisted living. We know it as giving cheerfully—trusting it will come back, perhaps not as quickly as if we had a fast-acting grandpa, but it will come back somehow, some way. We know it as reaping what we sow. We know it as affirming that all belongs to God; we are but the guardians, the caretakers. WE know this, don't we?

Even so, sometimes it feels like my fingers are having to be pried open one by one. I am prone to hold on tightly to what I have, but the urging of God says: "Open up, expand your horizons to a deeper meaning of life."

Psalm 37 encourages the same kind of thing, encourages us to exchange tight-fisted living for what I am calling a horizonal kind of living—an opening wider of heart and soul.

Try something with me, would you please? Close your fists, both of them as tightly as you can. As I remind us of the suggestions from Psalm 37 about faithful living, unfold one finger at a time.

Trust in the Lord
Do good
Take delight in the Lord
Commit your way to the Lord
Be still before the Lord
Wait patiently
Do not fret over those who prosper or carry out evil
Refrain from anger
Forsake wrath
Do not fret; it only leads to evil (interesting—that is
in there twice)

Open hands—do you feel the difference? Open hands is an old, old way of praying. In fact, it was the kind of praying the earliest Christians used, as well as those in other religious traditions. Hands open and wide indicate a willingness to surrender and to receive the gifting of God.

As I stand here with my hands and arms opened wide, I am reminded of Julie Andrews in the "Sound of Music." Remember her standing on the mountain with her hands and arms and heart open wide? [I turn around in the chancel.] She was experiencing an openness to the beauty of God's presence.

I have had that same kind of Julie Andrews experience in the Panhandle of Texas. Now don't laugh. People usually laugh when I say there is a wonderful beauty to the Texas Panhandle. I suspect you may have to have been born there to truly appreciate it, but it's there in all its flatness. Big sky—no hills—no trees—nothing to get in the way of sky and land meeting, and that wide horizon stretching so far that you can begin to see the curve of the earth. Yes, you can. There is something in my soul that needs a wide-open horizon stretching out in front of me. From time to time I need a horizon to remind me that the world and life are bigger than my house...my neighborhood...my routine...my particular chaos.

A far-reaching horizon reminds me there is a width and a breadth that I forget in my clenched, tight-fisted day-to-day living. I forget that we are made for "horizonal living"—openly receiving the gifting of God.

It doesn't have to be a trip to Texas or the mountains to stretch the horizon of life. It can happen in a moment, in a conversation, in a flash of insight that says, "Here is a wider experience of life."

I will never forget seeing one of those horizonal moments happen in someone's life. It was a pastor's class. Fifth graders were preparing to be baptized and to become full members of the church. One of our lessons was about stewardship. We talked about stewardship as lifestyle and about how the giving of ourselves to Christ included our money. Copies of the church's budget were handed out so that the learners could glimpse the width and variety of ministries made possible by persons' giving, by their own giving. Donnie looked over the budget carefully, noting our outreach ministries, education budget, evangelism budget, youth ministries, administrative budget. I could see the moment that Don saw a new horizon— his eyes widened to a new and broader perspective. He said, "Hey, you mean the money I give pays your salary?" I was so pleased that he had made a tangible connection. I was so flattered that he saw my salary as an important aspect of the church's wider ministry. That's when he said, "Well then, you better straighten up!"

That moment expanded my horizons too!

Horizonal moments—when a broader perspective becomes clearer and a wider view of the world and your place in it comes into focus.

The Week of Compassion is one expression of the church's stewardship; and it is a horizon-expanding moment in the life of the church—a moment when we pry open the fingers of our daily doings, and we are urged to stretch wide, joining our hands with the hands of others: other churches and other denominations. Hands that are joined widely enough to reach all around the world.

Stewardship living does that. It takes us far beyond paying a poor preacher, far beyond a church budget, far beyond a drive in the Texas Panhandle, even far beyond one moment of insight. Stewardship living and an offering like Week of Compassion launches us into space where we can see that the horizon is really a circle. The straight line before us is a part of the entire world creating a perfect wholeness and unity of life.

I would rather hold on tightly to what I have, but the urging of God says: "Open up. Expand your horizons to a deeper meaning of life—all of life." What begins as my money...my life...my house...my church are transformed into God's world...God's sky and land embracing one another...God's church...God's neighborhood...my life and money—God's, committed and entrusted to God. It's a mysterious thing. We call it stewardship—horizonal living. It opens our lives to receive the amazing gifting of God. I want to hold on tightly to what I think I have, but the hope of God urges: "Open up. Expand your horizons—experience a deeper meaning of life."

$\mathcal{T}$HE QUESTION OF COMPASSION

David L. Welsh

> *The statistics in this sermon can be overwhelming,
> and the preacher recognizes this. He capitalizes on the
> overwhelming nature of statistics regarding poverty
> and uses them to help move from being overwhelmed
> to a more positive approach to assisting others. It also
> affirms the great "perhaps" that opens the possibility of
> God's amazing activity for healing and hope in the world.*

John 6:1–14

Probably no scene in the life of Jesus is more familiar; indeed, it is the one miracle recorded in all four Gospel accounts. The multitude has followed Jesus—heard him teach, seen his miracles—and so, here beside the Sea of Galilee, they have come for more. The day has passed quickly, and now as evening approaches, Jesus looks across the sea of hungry faces, and turns to his Disciples and asks: How are we to buy bread, so that these people may eat?

How are we to feed all these hungry people?

During these weeks leading to the celebration of Easter, I have begun a series of sermons from the Gospel of John—a series not based on the "seven signs," one usual way of understanding this Gospel. Nor are they sermons intended more fully to explain Jesus' remarkable teachings—and they are indeed remarkable! Instead, the series will come from the *questions recorded in John that Jesus asked.* There are twenty-one such questions—each there to challenge, to encourage, and to push us farther in our journey of faith growth and its development.

Last week we turned to look at the very first words of Jesus as recorded in the Gospel of John. It is that remarkable question addressed to us individually, calling for our personal, honest commitment and response. Jesus asks, "What are you looking for?"

David L. Welsh is pastor of First Christian Church in Wilson, North Carolina.

What do we really want from life? From God? What do we want for ourselves, and for our world? What are we looking for?

Now, I know that we do not ever finally answer that question—or perhaps, it is better to say, this is a question that we have to address over and over again. Hopefully, during this Lenten Season, we can take more seriously the implications it places upon us: What are we really looking for? That, first.

Today, the second question, the words of Jesus to his disciples, How are we to buy bread so that these people may eat? And then, as John states in the very next verse, "This Jesus said to test him."

And it is a most unusual test!

Think for a moment, not about that hillside nearly two thousand years ago, but think about what Jesus sees as he looks out across our world today. We'd have to confess, there are still hungry people!

Of a world population of just over six billion, nearly 470 million (or one person in twelve) faces not just hunger but life-threatening starvation. Probably an additional one billion are badly undernourished and take in hardly enough calories even to exist. The facts are staggering: nearly forty thousand die each day, not because of war or disease or natural disaster, but simply because they don't have a portion of daily bread.

Yes, Jesus looks at the multitude and he still sees *hungry people!* And, in faith, we are forced to look as well. As we sit in our comfortable chairs in well-heated dens, the color TV presents a face: the face of a child, hollow, dark eyes; a shriveled frame, emaciated, stomach bloated. And the announcer tells us that if all the world's needy children were to line up thirty-six inches apart outside our front door, the line would encircle the globe...twenty-five times. Twenty million die each year of starvation. Half are children!

We look, but we turn our eyes to the picture of our own family there on the wall, and we think about our obligations: rent and groceries, bills to be paid, college tuition and prom night expenses...and so we would reach to change the channel....

Only, for a moment, we feel frozen. It is as if Jesus touches our hand, our heart—and he speaks again his word: *How are we to buy bread so that these people may eat?* Our faith is tested, indeed, like those first disciples—tested not by what we say, but by what we do.

It is interesting that in John's Gospel the author goes on to give us two examples. First, there is Philip. He responds the way most of us would respond; he is pragmatic, practical. "Jesus," he says, "there are so many people, and we have so little money—what are we to do?"

His answer is realistic. Honest. He was not a callous man. He probably felt deeply about the people and their situation. But the magnitude of the problem was simply too great. Immobilized by the size of the crowd, he shook his head in despair.

How are we going to feed these hungry people? Philip said: *No way.* But Andrew said: Lord, perhaps….And it was his "perhaps" that opened up the possibility for the miracle to take place. Yes, only five loaves and two fish, but there was also the power of Christ. And so the multitude was fed—"filled," John says, filled to overflowing!

Jesus looks at our world, and he still sees hungry, hurting, homeless, helpless people. And he asks a question that tests our faith: *How are we going to feed them? How are we going to meet their needs?*

If we are practical and pragmatic, we will have to conclude, like Philip, It's just not possible. There are too many people and not enough bread. But if we can believe like Andrew, believe that by giving what we can, to be used by the power of Christ, then perhaps… just perhaps….

This day we receive gifts to our church's effort to meet those enormous needs throughout the nations of our world today: to refugees, to those with no homes, no schools, not even the "luxury" of water to drink.

It is our Week of Compassion offering. Before us is the goal of raising $2,800,000 nationwide—and for this congregation, our share, $4,000. Twenty-three percent of the monies received will be used for immediate emergency aid—for victims of earthquakes, famine, the "natural disasters" (that the insurance companies have so wrongly named "acts of God"). Sixteen percent is designated to refugee resettlement support. Thirty-nine percent is intended for preventative programs of education and self-help development. You have heard the phrase: "Give a man a fish and he will eat for a day; teach a man to fish and he will eat for a lifetime." This 39 percent is for that kind of teaching and long-term improvement.

Food, water, medicine, farm equipment, seeds, schools— all sorts of fishing poles and lessons on how to use them—they account for 94-95 percent of every dollar received. Less than 6 percent goes into the administrative and delivery costs—and for those who know anything about charitable giving, you know that it is fair to say that no dollars that you ever give will go as far and do as much as these in our Week of Compassion offering.

And why do we give?

Let me be clear: The sermon isn't intended to make anyone feel guilty about the situation of the poor, and so encourage them to give. As I said from this pulpit three weeks ago, "Guilt should never be the motivation for our Christian behavior." Our giving is instead a response to Christ's question, a response born of hope.

The question in this sixth chapter of John is not a question about hunger. It is a question of compassion, one that asks us to examine what we believe about Jesus, his power, and the possibility that lies within us, no matter the size of our gift.

It is a question that tests our faith, for how we respond begins to measure the size and the hope of our believing. It is a question about our compassion: Will we give up in face of the enormity of the problem? Will we give up?

Or will we give? Give what we can? To be used, blessed, and become the starting point of the miracle that God would do in the midst of our hungry world.

RIDGING THE GAP

John R. Compton

> *Stewardship of resources is an act of bridge-building.*
> *Bridging the gap between those whose resources are limited*
> *and those whose resources are adequate is necessary. In*
> *order to enter into that, most must feel the weight of the*
> *need of the other. By the giving of our Reconciliation*
> *offering we connect with the unexplored in God's world*
> *and contribute to the divine process of healing.*

2 Corinthians 5:18–19

We dream of a whole world; we see a fragmented world. We experience an epileptic world. We live in a broken world. Our world is characterized by broken relationships. The world we know is one where estrangement among social classes is common and where racism tends to make life narrow and bitter. So ours is a world filled with violence, stupidity, greed, isolation, blindness, and despair. Healing needs to happen, because God's world is made for personal relationships among persons and their God, and among persons on this earth. God sent Christ into the world to reconcile persons to each other and to their God. God was in Christ, reconciling the world to himself, and entrusting to us the message of reconciliation. So we are ambassadors for Christ.

In the letter to the Ephesians, Paul wrote: "We, being rooted and grounded in love, may have power"—to develop relationships that have height and depth and length and breadth to bridge the gaps that separate us from one another. It is no easy task, this function of reconciling love, this bridging of the

In "retirement," John Compton pastors St. John's Christian Church in Cincinnati, Ohio. He has served in many leadership capacities among Disciples, including the presidency of the Division of Homeland Ministries. He is a former administrative director of Reconciliation, the focus of this sermon.

gaps in so-called Christian America. But humankind has accomplished hard tasks—seemingly impossible ones—across the centuries. One of these tasks is bridge-building.

Webster defines a bridge as a structure providing passage over a waterway, a valley, a road, or other gap or barrier, without closing the way beneath. Let us consider the George Washington Bridge over the Hudson River. Connecting 179th Street in New York City with Fort Lee, New Jersey, the bridge was completed more than sixty years ago and has been carrying traffic since October 1931. The bridge was built with eight railway tracks, a roadway, and two footpaths. It was built with 26,474 wires in each cable, which helps to give it support. The bridge was under construction for four and one-half years.

Building Bridges Is a Challenge

To build the George Washington Bridge called for skill, ingenuity, finance, and above all, will. Many thought it was an impossible task. So, too, bridging the gaps in our personal and social relationships often seems an impossible task. But Christians, inspired by faith in God, are not ready to admit that we lack the skill, the ingenuity, the finances, the will to bridge these human gaps.

While it is no easy task—this function of reconciling love, this bridging of the gaps—it is a task that Christ has given to his followers. "God was in Christ, reconciling the world to himself," and God has made us—each of us—agents of reconciliation.

We have this ministry. We are to build bridges across poverty pockets, cultural chasms, and racial rivers. We are called by God to be involved in reconciling ministries. Urban America, especially the inner cities of our nation where racism, poverty, and broken fellowships are rampant, offers the church a tremendous opportunity to be involved in reconciling ministries.

The Plight of the Inner City

Will you join me now for an excursion through the inner city? Persons from minority groups are stacked and jammed in this less-favored part of the metroplex. Inner-city humanity lives in a ghetto—economic, racial, cultural—frequently all three. They are frequently jobless, with few employment possibilities because they possess few marketable skills. They are undereducated or miseducated. The high school dropout rate is the highest in the city. The area in which they live is often cited for its juvenile delinquency and crime. The schools are overcrowded, understaffed or poorly staffed, old, and in need of repairs.

Inner city residents are the victims of inadequate housing, for which they pay exorbitant rent. Housing in these broken-down, dreary, and defeated communities is overcrowded. Residents may live in cold-water flats that must be shared with rats and roaches. Housing and building codes are seldom enforced. Persons have become accustomed to seeing filth, garbage, and trash in the streets and junk in vacant lots.

Loan companies take advantage of people in the inner city. So do automobile agencies and supermarkets. Residents often pay higher rates of interest and higher food prices than persons who live in more affluent parts of the city.

Inner city residents find themselves victims of police stares, questionings, and sometimes brutality. The children often suffer from the breakdown of family life. The inner city has more than its share of mothers with children and roving males. Playground and recreation centers are inadequate. In short, inner city dwellers often have the most of everything bad and the least of anything good.

Modern-day Lepers

People in the inner city are lonely, frustrated, rootless, isolated and alienated. They are the lepers of modern society, living in a kind of leprosarium—the inner city. Should we be surprised that they often turn to alcohol, prostitution, gambling, narcotics, stealing, and sometimes violence as they seek a means of escape?

Our nation's inner cities offer us a challenge and an opportunity to involve ourselves in reconciling ministries to help meet the special needs of the poor, powerless, voiceless, and culturally deprived—the racially alienated and the underprivileged whites. It is a challenge and an opportunity to build bridges.

The Weight of the Cross

The story is told of some American tourists, a husband and wife, who went to see the famous Passion Play at Oberammergau. They were visiting with the actor who was playing the part of Christ, just as he was preparing for the scene in which the Via Dolorosa to Calvary is portrayed.

The woman turned to her husband and said, "Why don't we take a picture of you with the cross?" With permission from the actor, the man bent to lift the cross on his back, but it was too heavy. "Why, in heaven's name, did you make it so heavy?" he asked. "One made of papier-maché would look as good."

The actor replied, "Sir, I could not play the part of Christ if I did not feel the weight of his cross."

We cannot serve as Christ's ambassadors in reconciling the world to God until we've felt the weight of his cross.

Like bridge building, reconciliation is risky, heavy business. Christians must take the risk and lift the weight if we are to bridge the gap. God has called us to participate in his ministry of reconciling love through the use of our talents, time, and money. Will we at least be wires that help sustain the Reconciliation bridge over troubled waters for the troubled of our world? God has called...God awaits our answer. What will be our response?

*H*IS WHOLE SELF

Maureen A. Dickmann

> *Rarely do we think of stewardship as a focus of funeral sermons. However, there is no question that a eulogy frequently reflects the management of resources that was inherent in the life of the deceased. The preacher of this sermon reflected stewardship in concrete terms. This is an important task for us who tend to speak only in ideas. The word became flesh, and it is important for us to share human stories of faithful living so that others might model their own lives around such stories.*

Malachi 3:10; James 2:14–17; Psalm 23; John 12:24–26

[I can think of no more powerful sermon on stewardship than the life and witness of one particular individual, a layman named Woody Whitlow. His life had been profoundly affected by learning from personal experience about what he liked to call the "joy of giving." He came to know that his faith was strengthened and deepened the more he gave. He liked to talk about how giving was so important, "not because the church needs it, certainly not because God needs it, but because I need to give. What giving does for me couldn't be accomplished any other way—all the riches of the world couldn't gain it for me."

Woody was not shy about sharing this message with others, both in his words and his example. His funeral, then, was an opportunity to reflect on the impact this particular steward had on so many people. After this sermon celebrating Woody's witness and encouraging us to carry on his spirit, an individual in our congregation who had been recalcitrant about serving in a particular way changed his mind and agreed to do it, unable to resist any longer in the face of Woody's testament.]

Our Gospel reading today is taken from the Gospel According to John. Jesus is speaking to his disciples, and he says, "Truly I say to you, unless a grain of wheat falls into the earth

Maureen Dickmann is pastor of Rock Bridge Christian Church in Columbia, Missouri.

and dies, it remains alone, but if it dies, it bears much fruit.
Those who love their lives above all else ultimately lose them,
but those who give their lives in this world will keep them for
eternal life. Those who serve me must follow me and where I
am, there shall my servants be also. God who loves me will
honor those who serve me."

We are gathered here this beautiful morning to celebrate
and give thanks for the life of a remarkable man; a man who
has touched each one of our lives; a man who has, by the way
he lived his life, evoked the tremendous response you see here
today—the outpouring of love and admiration, the genuine
respect so many have expressed, the deep affection felt, that
makes this parting so difficult.

You can read the newspaper and learn he was a son and a
brother; that he served his country as a soldier and married the
woman he loved; that he worked in the world as a credit manager, but he gave his heart and soul to the church of Jesus Christ;
that he leaves behind as a legacy numerous nephews and nieces,
grandnephews and grandnieces, and their children; and that he
also leaves behind as a legacy a whole community of friends—
from the Lenoir community and the volunteer sector, whether
it's Regional Hospital or Meals on Wheels or all the many other
ways he served—and most of all, his church community.

Woody was a man who loved the church and served it in
every way possible: serving in the "upper reaches" (if you will)
on the General Board of the Christian Church (Disciples of
Christ), serving on the board of Week of Compassion, serving
the Mid-America Region's Northeast Area of the Christian
Church (Disciples of Christ) in so many ways—on the board,
as treasurer of the Area, as chairperson of the Sharing the
Spirit campaign that recently ended. At the level of the local
church, he was unsurpassed in his devotion. At Memorial Boulevard in St. Louis, he served in so many ways: a long-time
elder, a long-time Sunday school teacher.

In 1980, he and Mildred uprooted themselves from a much-
beloved community in St. Louis, especially from that church.
You see, Woody retired that year, and he was no sooner retired
than he was looking to the future, planning the best use of his
time and his gifts. And that plan included Lenoir and Columbia. Mildred will be the first to tell you, she came kicking and
screaming, but come she did. And very soon it became clear
that God needed them here in a very special way.

You see, there was a plan to start a Disciples church in
the south part of Columbia. The Whitlows were approached

about being a part of that new church, and the rest is history. Not that it was all smooth sailing, but over the long haul of thirteen-plus years, through the ups and through the downs, Woody has been the driving force of this little church, Rock Bridge. His imprint is all over it—in the unusual commitment to outreach giving and in the personal service to those in need and, just as importantly, in the warmly enthusiastic welcome each visitor to this church receives. So a very important part of the legacy Woody leaves is the community of faith known as Rock Bridge Christian Church. He was clearly the father of this church. He carefully nurtured so many things about it; just by his example showing what it meant to be a Disciple of Christ, both with a capital "D" and with a small "d." In his tireless efforts, he showed us all what it means to reach out to the "least of these," Christ's brothers and sisters. No one was ever too poor, too lowly, too unacceptable to receive Woody's generous touch.

But you know what? Woody would not want me to be talking about him today. To him, he wasn't so noteworthy; just let him get on with whatever task he was about and don't make any "to-do" about it. No big deal. Woody would want us to dwell today on the good news of Jesus Christ and forget Woody Whitlow.

The thing is, though, that he incarnated the good news of Jesus Christ so much in the way he lived his life, it is hard to talk about one without the other. Woody was a prism through which the love of God showed so clearly that it lit up the lives of those he touched. How did he do that? In the course of our conversations these past days, Mildred has asked me several times, "They loved him so much—why? What is it about him?" I think one of the keys was something I heard over and over again last night at the visitation: Woody was somebody who put his *whole self* into everything he did. Woody was a man who was "out there." You knew where he stood, what he thought, who he was, every moment, every day. This was illustrated to me early on. Even before I really knew him.

I had accepted the call to come to Rock Bridge and was living in New Haven, Connecticut, at that time. So moving me out here became the next issue. We investigated the cost of a professional mover; it was very high. So knowing Woody as you all do, you know what happened next. "We'll move her ourselves!" And sure enough, he flew up to New Haven. I picked him up at the airport in the late afternoon and took him back to my place, where I had about a dozen friends helping me load the truck I had rented. He, of course, as you would expect, pitched in and loaded more than anybody else by the end of the evening. At one point we ordered pizzas and sat around eating them. You know, Woody never met a stranger, and he got to know all those folks. There was one woman in particular who was impressed by him. I had worked with her in the retirement community where I was the chaplain for three years. She was a young Jewish woman, a reaction therapist, who was not easily impressed. At the end of the evening she called me aside and she said, "You know, I *like* that Woody! He's just so…I don't know…I just even like the way he eats his pizza!"

The next morning, he got up at 5:00 a.m. and drove straight through from New Haven to St. Louis—about 1,300 miles. He did tell me recently that the rental truck had "quite a bit of pep" for a rental truck! (I can imagine he didn't quite stay under the speed limit the whole way.) He got to Mildred's sister's in the middle of the night about ready to drop, but by God, I was *moved*! It's a story about Woody Whitlow that's typical. When you need something done, Woody's the man for the job!—putting his whole self into it.

I keep trying to get away from dwelling on Woody too much, but it's impossible. The truth is that talking about Woody's life and who he was is basically talking about the gospel. He'd dismiss the idea, I'm sure, but the man did live out a life of discipleship that is unmatched in my experience. He was a person eager—as we say in the Twelve Step Program—not only to talk the talk, but was even more committed to walking the walk. That phrase about "walking the walk" is a very apt one about Woody; it is more than a metaphor in his life.

Each spring he walked twenty miles in the Memorial Boulevard "Week of Compassion Hike." Many of us in this room today sponsored him, no doubt, for that walk through the years. Last year's hike was unbelievable. He had been through six months of chemotherapy and radiation that might have killed a lesser man. He got us all to sponsor him, saying, well, he was "going to try it," maybe he'd do only a few miles, "maybe ten miles"—he'd just do what he could do. But I knew when I signed my pledge that I was going to pay for twenty miles! He not only finished that hike, he spurred others on.

Johnny Wray, the director of Week of Compassion, came to walk with Memorial this year. He started the hike out enthusiastically, but after about five miles his feet were hurting and he was wanting to quit; and here was Woody Whitlow, seventy-five years old, just through with six months of chemotherapy, marching on and keeping him marching on. Isn't that just the way Woody was? Not only pushing himself, but spurring others along.

Woody was always open to learning more, finding his "growing edges," as we say. Woody and I explored some of those growing edges (for each of us) together. When I came here over seven years ago, he was pretty sure he was as enlightened as he needed to be about women in the church. After all, he had been married to Mildred forty-five years at that time, and what more could he need to know?

As Woody and I got to know each other and learned in ministry together, it became clear there were areas where we needed to "understand each other better" (I couldn't find a more diplomatic word). One thing about Woody was that he was unafraid to state his position, as you all know very well, and yet he was also remarkably unafraid to be open to another person's position, to listen and to try to understand. He made me grow because of his willingness to grow.

It's hard to believe that only ten weeks ago, Woody Whitlow stood at this lectern and preached our thirteenth anniversary service about how he had seen the face of God in a variety of other people. And as he recounted all of his experiences, I know I wasn't the only one in this room thinking of all the times that I had looked at that face of God in him. He wouldn't want to hear about it, but I think that all of us folks gathered here today caught a glimpse of that face of God he was so ready to see in others, but was sometimes reluctant to see in himself.

For those of us who loved him and have such a hard time letting him go, let us remember that our most meaningful expression of love for him is following his example—to love as he loved, to find ways of serving others as he did, to put our whole selves into everything we do. His legacy to us is great. The only suitable response is to pick up where he left off, carrying on his vision. He loved that quote, "The church exists by mission as a flame exists by burning." For him, it wasn't only true for the church but for persons too; we only exist by serving others, by giving of ourselves. To follow that example is the greatest tribute we can give.

Now, his time of serving and giving is over; he has been gathered in the arms of his Lord, and now he can rest in peace. Amen.

*E*XTRAORDINARY *L*IFE *P*OLICIES

Rhodes Thompson

> *Not enough sermons are preached on this topic. This
> sermon is an upfront challenge for people to leave their
> accumulated resources to the ministry of life for the future.
> Deeply moving testimony reflects courageous living by the
> preacher. Stories of ordinary people who placed their
> resources in the hands of extraordinary ministries reveal
> the radical difference commitment can make. We preachers
> must preach more sermons like this!*

A friend once wrote asking to visit Robert Louis Stevenson,
having heard he was very sick and in danger of dying. Quickly
came this reply, "By all means come, not to see one who is in
danger of dying, but to see one who is in danger of living!"

Many who fear the danger of dying have taken out "ordinary life policies" so as not to leave their loved ones destitute
if they should die prematurely. However, those who take Jesus
at his word face the prospect not of dying but of living: "I am
the resurrection and the life. Those who believe in me, even
though they die, will live, and everyone who lives and believes
in me will never die" (John 11:25–26). Death for them involves
changing residence into those wider ranges of the soul that we
call heaven. Therefore, before that great moving day comes,
and as a loving way of touching and blessing their global family, this sermon challenges Christians to consider the joys of
taking out "extraordinary life policies."

By doing that, William Garth, a member of my home
church in Paris, Kentucky, found an extraordinary way to
be a continuing part of the life of Bourbon County. Upon his
death in 1860, his will allocated $42,612.20 for a fund whose

---

Rhodes Thompson has retired to Claremont, California, after a lifetime of ministry in
pastorates, overseas missions (Japan), and seminary teaching (Phillips Theological Seminary). He is the author of *Stewards Shaped by Grace* (Chalice Press), and is in wide
demand as a seminar leader on Christian stewardship.

interest would help Bourbon County boys get a college education. Between 1946 and 1950, $1,000 from that fund helped me attend Texas Christian University, paying for a lot of tuition at the going rate of ten dollars per semester hour! In 1988, the corpus of that Garth Fund had grown to $180,050.52, and its interest of $89,614 for 1984-1988 alone was twice as much as the amount of the original endowment. As it was said of Abel, so can it be said of William Garth, "He died, but through his faith he still speaks" (Hebrews 11:4)—and educates boys.

Then, in 1952, when I entered Lexington Theological Seminary, yet another Garth Fund provided my full tuition for three years of seminary education. Only this time the benefactor was Claude Garth, a Christian layman from Scott County, Kentucky, who left $90,606.93 in a fund to help students for the ministry. Though he joined the communion of the saints in 1905, "through his faith he still speaks." By 1988 that original endowment had grown to $127,444, meanwhile producing $535,000 of interest to help educate hundreds of ministers and missionaries—and the end is not yet. As long as the church continues, Mr. Garth will continue to help provide professional leadership for the church. The barrel of meal does not waste away, and the cruse of oil does not fail when dedicated to the Lord's work as Mr. Garth so wisely dedicated his estate.

Two men named Garth; two wills designated $133,219.13 for educational purposes, whose combined principals totaled $307,494.52 in 1988; thousands of people directly and indirectly blessed since 1860 and 1905; and more than $30,000 of interest annually available for these purposes "in perpetuity." Just imagine the lost blessings to church and world if those two wills had not been written! Assuredly the Garths' great generosity has produced thanksgiving to God, "for the rendering of this service not only supplies the wants of the saints but also overflows in many thanksgivings to God" (2 Corinthians 9:11–12, RSV). Now, imagine the great danger of our own Christian living; namely, forgetting to take out our own extraordinary life policies so that God may be honored and people blessed in the church and world after our "roll is called up yonder"!

Challenged by that exposure to the meaning of the legal instrument called a will, I preached my first sermon on that subject in Daytona Beach on September 22, 1957. In that sermon were these words: "Note well: My own preparation for the preaching of this sermon has involved my own personal act of consulting a lawyer and drawing up a will!" In each succeeding decade, Lois and I have rewritten our wills. As we prepared to leave for Japan, our Division of Overseas Ministries convinced us that Lois and I should have separate wills, even though each might be essentially the same. Changes in family situation and place of residence often make revision and updating of wills advisable. This I have learned after agonizing with families about wills that, for lack of updating, actually worked against the original intent of their writers.

Furthermore, I believe it is important to find a competent, trustworthy lawyer to help draft a will. It is also essential to make your own sense of Christian stewardship clear to that lawyer so that you are in charge of substantive decisions, with her/him providing the needed professional advice and assistance. If you do not know such a lawyer, seek guidance from local, regional or general offices of your church.[1] The cost of writing a will with reputable assistance pales in comparison to the costs that will be claimed for legal fees if you die intestate. This, too, I have learned from observation. The peace of mind that comes from planning how you want your affairs and resources handled in the event of your death is beyond calculation. The state's formula for settling your estate, if you leave no will, contains no provision for the church nor for fulfilling your Christian faith and desires. That is your business, and no one else's. Beware of the danger of living without life policy!

So let us dare to be specific without absolutizing our experience for anyone else. The way Lois and I have written our Christian wills fits us but may not fit you and your situation. Nevertheless, perhaps these ideas will prompt your own creative reflection. An important part of our wills in earlier years involved naming guardians for our children and setting up a plan for using our family resources to help with their care and education. Now our children are on their own, and that is reflected in the shape our wills have taken. Three major provisions are worth mentioning:

(1) In the event of my prior death, all our accumulated resources will go to Lois for her continued management in accordance with our standards of Christian stewardship. If Lois predeceases me, all those resources will come to me.

(2) In the event Lois and I die in a common disaster, all our financial assets will become part of a trust fund to be managed by our three children, with our son bearing chief legal responsibility, since he is a graduate of Columbia Law School. (When our children were younger, we had named the Christian Church Foundation to manage this fund.) They will be

responsible for investing or depositing these funds, which means they probably will not offer the highest dividends or interest. For twenty years interest from this trust fund will be annually divided in equal portions among our children. Two main purposes will be achieved in this way: our resources will undergird socially useful programs while they are invested or deposited; and after twenty years each of our children will have received an amount of interest comparable to one-third of our estate at the time of our deaths by common disaster.

(3) Twenty years after both of us or the last of us dies, the total trust fund will be divided equally among six Christian ministries: two that are educating ministers to bring God's vision to God's people in the church, Phillips Theological Seminary and Lexington Theological Seminary; two that are engaged in Third World ministries helping people help themselves and others, Division of Overseas Ministries of the Christian Church (Disciples of Christ) and Habitat for Humanity; and two that are involved in the work of peace and justice domestically and globally, American Friends Service Committee and Fellowship of Reconciliation.

We believe our will provides us a way of loving both our own family *and* our global family in the church and in the world. We believe our children are themselves global in their interests and affections. We believe they will use the resources we leave them for good in their lives and in our world. And we believe the six Christian ministries mentioned above are eminently qualified to make the most of our accumulated resources in honoring God and blessing people in accordance with God's purpose set forth in Christ.

Do you begin to see what I mean by "extraordinary life policies?" That way of speaking imbues the term "will" (our legal way of carrying out our wishes after our deaths) with a new quality of life. Without denying death's reality, it affirms Jesus' promise that "whoever lives and believes in me shall never die" (John 11:26, RSV). Jesus' Parable of the Rich Fool is poorly understood as God's words to us on our deathbeds: "Fool! This night your soul is required of you; and the things you have prepared, whose will they be?" (Luke 12:20, RSV). Surely Jesus sought to push the import of that question forward in time for us who are very much alive. And the things you are presently managing, whose are they now? In either case, the answer is the same, whatever the tense of the question: they are God's—and we are responsible for using them to honor God and bless people. There is a timelessness about that answer and that responsibility for those called to be stewards of God's varied grace.

That sense of timelessness marked the stewardship of Alfred Avery, a devout Christian industrialist who sponsored the Parshad Scholarship Contest through the United Christian Youth Movement in 1946, the year I finished high school. As the fortunate national boy's winner that year, I received scholarship aid for college ($1,600 over the next four years) and for UCYM conferences in Tennessee, Colorado, and Michigan. Best of all, I received the friendship of Alfred Avery and his wife, Ethel, and the chance to hear and experience their remarkable life story.

As a teenager Alfred Avery determined a plan for his life. During the first twenty years he would get all the education he could. On target in reaching that goal, as a college graduate he went to work for the Dupont Company. The next twenty years he would make all the money he could. On target again, remunerated by salary and by company stock, greatly appreciated in value, he was independently wealthy by the age of forty. However, wisely, he and his wife, Ethel, had decided on a plan to keep money from owning them during those money-making years. Beginning by tithing, they increased their giving by 5 percent of their income every five years: at age twenty-five to 15 percent, at thirty to 20 percent, at thirty-five to 25 percent. At forty, as they talked about their next increase, Ethel suddenly said, "Alfred, we could live on the 25 percent, so why don't we give 75 percent!" So that is what they began doing.

At forty his plan also involved resigning from whatever work he was then doing in order to spend the rest of his life using his time, talents, and treasure at God's beck and call. The best Dupont could do in dissuading him from his plan was to keep him as a consultant. In following years, that remarkable man created some twenty small industries, directing profits from each to the support of the church and of charities. By the time he died in his early seventies, he and Ethel had given away more than $5,000,000!

In 1953, Lois and I had visited the Averys at their home in Hingham Bay, Massachusetts. One day Alfred Avery took me to his office in Malden where he handed me a brown scrapbook on which was written, in embossed gold letters, the word "Dividends." He beckoned me to open it. As I did, I found on each page a manila envelope on which someone's name appeared. Leafing through the pages, I came at last to one bearing my name and containing an envelope with all my letters to the Averys since becoming part of the Parshad family seven years before. Glancing up, I saw the quiet, warm smile on that man's face that told me he had found the secret of being a steward of God's varied grace.

A further discovery of what Alfred Avery was about unfolded while Lois and I were in India in 1982. Recalling that *parshad* was an Indian word meaning "the gift of God," but realizing I had never asked a native of India to tell me more about that word, I posed the question. At first I was shocked, for no one seemed to know the word. Then suddenly a student's eyes sparkled as he repeated the word, correcting my accent and pronunciation. Soon we learned that *parshad* described a Hindu custom of bringing fruits of the harvest to the temple where the priest blessed them, then gave them back to the donor to be shared with others in the community. How wonderful! Alfred Avery had presented his gifts to God, who had blessed and returned them to him for sharing with his wider family in the church and world.

After Alfred and then Ethel Avery joined that great cloud of witnesses who surround us in the church, I lost contact with the Parshad Foundation. However, his extraordinary life policy was in force long before then, and I had been a beneficiary. He reminds me that giving is an indelible mark of Christians on both sides of the doorway called death.

---

[1] Christian Church Foundation (Disciples of Christ), P.O. Box 1986, Indianapolis, Indiana 46206-1986 (Telephone: [317] 635-3100) can offer such assistance. Their Congregational Planned Giving Resource Series includes Guidelines for Policies, Memorial Funds, Wills and Financial Planning, and a Supplementary Packet, and is valuable for use in congregational consciousness-raising and planning.

*L*ET GOD BE GOD

Robert R. Botkins

> *How about a stewardship sermon that frees you from anxiety? This sermon helps us by reminding us of our place in the scheme of things. Its call to service of God rather than the idols of our heart is powerful. Maybe we need a sermon now and then that speaks to those of us who are tempted to worship the institution we are called to lead.*

Matthew 6:33

As I have watched the dissolution of the once-powerful Soviet Union, I have been wondering what might have happened to Sergei Debov. Perhaps you read about him late last year. Dr. Debov is a 72-year-old microbiologist. For the past forty years, he has been in charge of the corpse of Vladimir Lenin. For nearly fifty years, the corpse has been on display at the wall of the Kremlin. Nearly three million visitors annually filed by this quasi-religious relic of the former U.S.S.R.

Every Monday and Friday, Debov examined the corpse. He refreshed the hands and face with embalming fluid. Color monitors constantly reported on the temperature and humidity around the body. A secret embalming compound replaced the water in the skin. No bacteria could invade the corpse as long as the temperature was a constant 16 degrees Celsius and the humidity stayed at 70 percent. Lenin's skin still appeared supple and natural looking. Theoretically, this tabernacle of clay could endure forever, sealed within its airtight glass sarcophagus.

I wonder what Debov thinks his life's work has amounted to. Certainly, he must have been highly admired just a few

Robert R. Botkins is president of Midway College in Midway, Kentucky, a Disciples institution affiliated with the Division of Higher Education. This sermon was delivered at the 1992 Disciples Development Conference.

years ago. Debov's tragedy is not that he was involved in an enterprise that failed. His tragedy, from a Christian perspective, is not that he was on the wrong side, but that he was employed in the service of idolatry.

The Soviets intended to create an illusion that the beloved corpse could not decay. They sought, in a sense, to create a sacramental experience in which the real presence of Lenin would incarnate the life of the socialist world. Biblical faith indicts every such idolatrous impulse. The foundation of faithful living before God is first and foremost to acknowledge that we mortals are dust, that every breath we draw is a gracious gift. That in the power of our own strength, we can do nothing.

> You turn us back to dust,
>   and say, "Turn back, you mortals."
> For a thousand years in your sight
>   are like yesterday when it is past....
> For all our days pass away under your wrath;
>   our years come to an end like a sigh.
> The days of our life are seventy years,
>   or perhaps eighty, if we are strong;
> even then their span is only toil and trouble;
>   they are soon gone, and we fly away.
>   (Psalm 90:3–4a, 9–10)

Let us now draw our first lesson from scripture. Scripture never teaches that it is sinful to be finite, to be limited, to be dependent. Nor is it sinful to *cope* with finitude or even, for a time, to excel. To strive for excellence, what the Greeks called *arete* (virtue), is praiseworthy. But the essence of sin is idolatry, which is a form of lying. Idolatry is the most insidious form of lying because it is the lie of self-deception. Adam and Eve deceived themselves into accepting the serpent's message: "It is possible to live without God." The lie of all lies is the bad-faith assumption that we are not finite, not ultimately dependent on a transcendent power.

Let us not assume that self-deception is indigenous to Communism. Arrogance, too, is a sin. Secular capitalism has raised lying and deception to an art form. Ours is an information age, not a truth-loving age. Do you ever watch closely the typical political interview on television? Interviewees often are not interested in examining ideas to determine the best policies. Rather, they often play cat-and-mouse games intended to make one another look foolish.

According to last month's *Harpers*, even college athletes are trained to handle the media. They all seem to memorize three or four canned answers, no matter what the question. The crucial point is never to make yourself, your team, your coach, or your school look bad.

Someone said that the art of selling is trying to get people to buy something that they don't want and don't need at a price that is more than it is worth. With that in mind, watch TV advertising seriously for a while. In the pitch for cars and beer and soap and perfume, I am constantly being told that I can be young, I must be sexy, I have to be cool, I must be vital—forever. All I need is the right product. My friends, it is all just another version of Lenin smiling serenely in his glass tomb.

Does any of this bear directly on the Disciples Development Conference? Or the church's ministry as a whole? I believe that it does. First, we all work for institutions. And institutions, just like states and persons, try to ensure their own immortality. That is my first and virtually all-consuming duty as a college president. I've got to keep Midway College going. And just like the Energizer, "going, and going, and going!" That's our job as development people. And we never get enough. Can anyone here imagine yourself saying this: "Now Mrs. Green, we appreciate your interest in our work. But compared to other needs in the church, we are in very good shape. For example, your million dollars of appreciated assets could help little, struggling Midway College so much...."

For our own peace of mind, we may need to confess that the world would not collapse if our agencies failed—closed shop. Sooner or later, they probably will. I can tell you one thing. Throughout our history, scores more Disciples colleges have failed than have survived. We take ourselves and our institutions far too seriously. Neither I nor Midway College is indispensable in the scheme of things. "Our years come to an end like a sigh. The days of our life are numbered." Sergei Debov is not the only person to make a god of his work.

The development officer or the pastor who acknowledges his or her finitude does not have to quit in despair. Rather, two wonderful things can happen. First, we can be free to do our best, and then let God be God. Our Lord said, "Do not worry about your life...but strive for the kingdom of God, and all that you need will be given to you as well." In the name of Jesus Christ, my friends, and to free yourself from all idolatry, believe in God and relax! Neither your self-preservation nor the preservation of your unit or region or institution or congregation is ultimately in your control. Let God be God!

The second wonderful thing that can happen is that we will be free—to some extent at least—from lying, from living a professional life of deception. All of us in the development business have our uniforms and our special manners. Why, with a trained eye, you can spot a development officer almost as quickly as an FBI agent. When we acknowledge that we and our jobs are ultimately in God's hands, we will continue to be charming and suave. We will continue to promote our agencies' sizzle just as much as we do their steak. But all of our work will be tempered and refined by the fact that our ultimate faith and loyalty are not to our institutions, but to God. When, by God's grace, we have stopped so much worrying and fretting, we will live out of truth and not out of falsehood. "Strive first for God's rule and God's justice, and everything else will be taken care of as well."

The gospel tells us that we do not raise and manage resources so that we can secure our institutions for eternity. Rather, we do this so eternity might break into our institutions. The incarnation of God into human history through Christ and his church is the ongoing act of reconciliation of people with God and of people with people. When we take earthly treasure and transform it into enlightened minds, into economic justice, into escape from pain and demonic spirits, into fellowship and peace among nations—and when we do so in patience and humility and honesty—we are no longer simply officers of development. We are servants of Jesus Christ: Jesus Christ who is not dead lying embalmed in a glass tomb, but Jesus Christ who is the risen Lord, son of the living God.

$\mathcal{M}$OVED BY VISION

Rita Nakashima Brock

> *What does the modern mind do with apocalyptic*
> *scripture? Usually it avoids it, but this sermon points to*
> *the power of such literature to call us to responsible use*
> *of ourselves. I am intrigued in our time by this sermon's*
> *challenge that immediate results may not be the basis*
> *for responsible stewardship of time and resources.*
> *Maybe preaching needs to lift up service to*
> *a future we do not expect to see.*

Daniel 7:9–14; Mark 13:24–32

Apocalyptic texts do not leap out as obvious resources for sermons on stewardship. It could be argued that the expectation of end times encourages passive waiting, rather than active participation in the work of the *basileia*, the community of God, translated as the "kingdom of God." The unlikeliness of the possibilities, however, intrigues me. To cast these texts as calls to stewardship requires first a new angle on the meanings of apocalyptic writing, then an examination of how these particular texts fulfill those meanings. The hermeneutical task can lead us to a fresh understanding of what it means to expect the end of time.

I. Background Information

Apocalyptic texts are often assumed to be predictions. The latest such assumption showed up this September 13 when a group waited for the rapture, based on calculations from the Book of Revelation. (A colleague of mine who heard about it after the fact mourned a lost opportunity to buy a lot of items cheaply.) However, if we insist on the predictive character of

Rita Nakashima Brock holds the Endowed Chair in Humanities at Hamline University in St. Paul, Minnesota, where she teaches in the Religion and Women's Studies departments. She is very active in the Christian Church (Disciples of Christ), currently serving as chairperson of the board of directors of the Division of Overseas Ministries.

apocalyptic writing, we are left with the question of why someone who supposedly lived during the Exile would have so inaccu-
rately portrayed the events and names of the time, as the writer
of Daniel did. A number of glaring historical inaccuracies, beginning with 1:1, the dating of the Babylonian exile, indicate the
writer's concern was not with literal history. In assuming the
writer her/himself to be intelligent and careful, I suggest the purpose of the text was not to predict events, but to depict a vision
that would give hope to people in dire circumstances. Elisabeth
Schüssler Fiorenza, in her work on Revelation, has suggested
that apocalyptic writing be seen as mythopoetic speech, as writing that presents an exciting, imaginative vision of a new reality.
The vision invites believers to participate in its arrival through
passionate faith, perseverance, and action.

Daniel and Mark are written to communities under political oppression. In each the sharpened dualism of the suffering of
the present and of hope in a new reality present a clear contrast
between the world of the hearers of the text and the writer's vision of the future. Most apocalyptic writing has an intense, urgent, angry tone, a tone understandable given the controlling
forces of oppressive dictatorships like Greece and Rome. If we
are unable to be angry about pain and oppression, we lack the
passionate love and hope that empower us to act for change, and
we fall into passivity, despair, or apathy. While Daniel and Mark
present dualisms as antagonistic, each also shows conflict medi-
ated through divine action in the sending of the human one. The
messianic triumphalism of the human one in Daniel is trans-
muted in the Gospels to a suffering messianism, such that suffering is not overcome, but embraced in the very life of God. This
mediation of opposites in Mark moves forward into a transformation of the cosmos and into hope for the disciples in the new
life of the *basileia*. This points to the redemptive power of God's
love to save and transform even the most evil and hopeless of
situations, a power at the center of all apocalyptic visions.

II. Interpretation

While many Christians today live under oppressive political systems, most Americans would have a hard time relat-
ing to the kind of oppression first-century Christians or Jews
experienced. There are, however, many kinds of pressures that
can alienate us and cause us to lose sight of our religious convictions. Conservative Christians see such pressures in the
rise of secular culture and the indifference toward religion
of so many in our society. Progressives see it in the growing

economic inequities of our society and the values of individual achievement and acquisition that govern our economic system. Still others see it in the despair engendered by the nuclear shadow and the fear, hostility, and economic bankruptcy encouraged by the arms race. Those who face such things as the alcoholism or drug abuse rate, the frequency of teen suicide, child abuse, and spouse battering, or simply the difficulty so many of us find in trying to communicate with those we love, can see that, despite our democracy, America is not the *basileia.*

Apocalyptic visions invite us to participate in the possibilities for a transformed future because we experience in our own hearts and lives within the church our hope for ourselves and all of God's people. They ask us to open our hearts to the pain and suffering of the world and to give out of our passionate convictions about the redemptive power of divine love. We give out of hope and love, not out of fear and guilt. To believe in a vision means to give to each other and to the world out of who we are, out of a positive conviction about our best, most caring, committed selves. We give out of the generosity of our spirits because we believe that what we do speaks most loudly about our most heartfelt faith and hope.

We also seek tangible results. Results are crucial. I prefer to be careful about giving to organizations. I like to see evidence that my money or time is effectively used. Responsible stewardship does mean paying attention to what happens, and our denomination is careful to report to us what happens to the money we send. I find it exciting to read reports from the Division of Overseas Ministries, the Church Finance Council, and Week of Compassion to see how many lives are touched by our giving to the larger church. I want to see results from my giving because I want control of what is mine. This is not necessarily bad, but I think the function of the apocalyptic vision is that it asks us to give of ourselves and to the world for different reasons.

There is a dimension of anger and punishment in apocalyptic texts, a judgment on the unsaved, but we are not asked to worry about that. Any self-righteous judgment that may happen is God's business. Our business as Christians is to live in the empowerment of the spirit and in the confidence that the love of God can transform even the most evil of evils. Ours is not only a confidence we think and say, but a confidence we live and feel through our own experience of the spirit of love in our lives. Hence we give of our time and money to the building of the *basileia* because not to do so would be a betrayal of our deepest, most passionately alive selves.

III. Examples and Illustrations

Many famous examples of those whose lives were empowered by a vision occur to me: Rosa Parks, Martin Luther King, Jr., Dorothy Day, Susan B. Anthony, and so forth. The list is huge. Each name is a testimony to the power an individual life can gain and the impact to a whole community when we live out of vision. Unlike the social policies, technology, and methods that help us make our visions actual, visions do not become obsolete. They inspire generation after generation with their gift of intelligence, compassion, and awe. Through inspiration and vision, we move from being victims of society and history to becoming creators of life in the community of God.

Using famous people as examples can inspire, but they can also alienate laypeople because such conviction and action seem far away from the lives of ordinary people. If we look at our own congregations, we can often find lives lived quietly, yet they are lives intensely moved by vision. So many give time and money to the life of the church.

Another way to convey this sense of vision occurs to me in a story I once heard a woman tell about how she kept vigil for days at the bedside of her dying mother. A friend asked her why she wore herself out doing this when her mother was so afflicted with Alzheimer's disease that she did not recognize her own family. It was painful to face the daily reality of this stranger who did not know her. She said, "I go to be with her because of who I am and what is important to me. She may not know me, but I know who I am, and who I am was born of the love she had for me. I cannot walk away from that love simply because it hurts to see her so lost to me." I remember a similar feeling as I watched my comatose and physically disfigured mother die of cancer. I could not have stayed away because to have done so would have been a betrayal of what I believe about faithfulness and love.

The brokenness of our world is our mirror. What we do to heal it and to witness to the power of the gospel are not so much in immediate results, but in whether the face we see in the mirror is our own or one that is shaped by the temporary success we seek in that broken world. To live fully out of our own best selves and to give to others from the wellspring of generosity that surges forth from our deepest joy and love—that is what the apocalyptic vision asks of us. It asks us to make the church a real witness of God's love and to trust that love to heal the fractured and oppressive powers that frighten us, even when the results may lie generations away, or even at the end of time.

*T*HAT *T*HEY *M*IGHT *D*O *B*ETTER *T*HAN *W*E

Timothy C. Diebel

> *There are ripe times—times when persons are ready to decide what to do with their lives and resources. This sermon begins with such a time—graduation—and teaches with finely crafted words. By use of parenting images, this sermon calls us to responsible care for the planet, the home we inherit and bequeath to our children.*

Psalm 8

It has felt wonderful, but strange for him, this last week or so at school. Ambitions and the excitement that fuels them have bubbled over into almost every conversation, along with plans for the summer and promises to get together. He's graduating, and the climate has somehow changed. Underclassmen have greeted him with a mixture of envy and reverence, and there's even a trace of respect in the way the teachers say his name.

It's wonderful, and yet there's an awkwardness about it as well. Something in it all has changed—the hallways that have formed the frame around so much of his life seem somehow different now and less his own, as if they suddenly belonged to someone else. It already feels like a memory, even though he has yet to leave it behind.

And now, lying out in the field behind the house, feeling the damp grass beneath his back and the night air across his face, he stares up at the stars through the blackness of the sky. Open, vast, waiting—limitless possibility, like the world he is poised to enter. He's prepared, primed, and ready, and yet still understandably afraid. What is his place in the midst of it all? he wonders to himself. Small, yet resourceful, powerful, and human—with all that that can mean. Lying there, face upward to the stars, he feels the questions all but lift him

Tim Diebel is senior pastor of First Christian Church in Des Moines, Iowa.

off the ground: Who is he to be, and what is he to do, and what's it all to mean?

As if by way of an answer, from some Sunday school lesson long since forgotten, come words that somehow drift to mind—words from the psalmist saying, "You have given him dominion over the works of your hands, and put everything under his feet." And a warmth from within overpowers the chill from the air; a smile creeps over his face and a confidence quiets his fears as his lips make the promise his own: "I have been given dominion, and everything is under my feet."

They are words that seem natural to this season of graduation, when days of preparation melt smoothly into ones of realization. These are days pregnant with impatience, potential, and self-confidence; heady days when it seems as though the world has just been waiting for us to arrive; days just ripe for words like those of the psalmist—words of authority, awareness, and ability. "You have been given dominion over all the works of God's hands; everything is under your feet." We can only pray that they are words he will grow to understand more sensitively and faithfully than the parents and grandparents and teachers and preachers from whose lips he heard them in the first place.

We listened to those words and heard in them permission—permission to use and digest, consume, and manipulate, as we saw fit. And God knows how we have seen fit. We have cut and we have dug; we have extracted and we have infused; we have mined and we have radiated; we have leached and we have polluted; we have incinerated and we have killed to the point of extinction, all precisely as we have seen fit, leaving us frighteningly little creation over which to exercise the dominion we have been given.

And it's frightening. What with the ecological and interpersonal jeopardy in which we find ourselves, it's hard to deny now that we've had the wrong idea. We have lived as creation's bullies, and there's little left to push around. What we had heard as "permission to consume" turns out to have been "responsibility to care for and sustain," and we can only pray that our children will do better; that they will not simply learn from our mistakes, but will understand afresh the words as they were intended to be heard: that creation exists for the glory of God, not for the gratification of people; and that we and they are children of God who had best live up to that name by *fostering* God's creative purposes, rather than *consuming* them.

As our children step out of these days to draw on the fresh, clean pages of tomorrow, let us pray that they understand the stewardship to which they are called—that they aren't just taking care of "stuff"; this is no cosmic garage sale to be picked and bargained over. This is God's creation for which they are called to care, and that is awesome work indeed.

It is work not unlike parenting, and we pray that ours of them will be a good example. There in the home we tend to the lives with which we've been entrusted, and we shape the directions that their potentials will take. We feed and tend and nurture, and stimulate the growth we hope they will achieve. Sometimes that means some discipline and even some pain, but it always has their growth as its aim.

As parents we do our best to keep them safe and protected from life's severer dangers, but we know that that can't mean dressing them in armor and locking them in a room, for safety is worthless if, in the process of being saved, they shrivel and rot from lack of growth. Our efforts must be in their best interests, not for the service of our own ends; but the most successful at it have learned that those who do the best job manage to accomplish both. There is room for pride in the process of it all, but pride in what they have become, not pride in what we've managed to control. But thanksgiving is the larger emotion we hope to justify feeling; gratitude that we have been more of a help than a hindrance, a food more than a poison— and it will take some work to see that it's so.

The stewardship of life, of "all the works of God's hands," is like the parenthood of children, or so we hope they might learn—more by our repentance than by our record. We have done poorly by our trust with the world, and painfully they will inherit the damage we have done to it; but hopefully they will inherit the lessons we have learned from it as well. Our dominion, like our parenthood, is not an achievement, we now know, but a gift—not an entitlement, but a trust. Like parenthood, it is caring and tending and respecting. It is understanding our oneness with creation, as well as our uniqueness—the rivers in our veins and the soil in our skin, the seeds in our loins and the rocks in our bones; it is remembering our common origin and our futures inseparably linked; it is discovering the joy of bringing out the best, and giving thanks for the awesome privilege to try.

O Lord, our Sovereign,
    how majestic is your name in all the earth!...
When I look at your heavens, the work of your fingers,
    the moon and the stars that you have established;

> what are human beings that you are mindful of them,
>   mortals that you care for them?
> Yet you have made them a little lower than God,
>   and crowned them with glory and honor.
> You have given them dominion over the works of your hands;
>   you have put all things under their feet....
> O Lord, our Sovereign,
>   how majestic is your name in all the earth!
>   (Psalm 8:1a,3–6,9)

Our dominion is purpose within the vastness, vocation in the midst of the possibilities, and trust in the face of the potential to abuse it. And somehow in the darkness, a warmth from within overpowers the chill from the air; a smile creeps over his face and a confidence quiets his fears as his lips make the promise his own: "I have been given dominion, and everything is under my feet." Dear God, for his sake, and for yours, sustain in him the wisdom to understand it; sustain them all, we pray, that they might do better than we.

$\mathcal{D}$OMINION OR DOMINATION?

Timothy N. Tiffany

> *This fresh and passionate approach to the stewardship of the earth is powerful. It reminds us of the relationship between dominion and community. We are bound together with that which we seek to dominate. How shall we struggle through the maze of economic development and ecological decency? This sermon contains some important thoughts for the future.*

Genesis 1:24—2:4a

Like being in a cathedral. Like being in church. Like hearing the "Hallelujah Chorus" on a sunny, bright Easter morning.

That was how I felt as we wandered down trails in Muir Woods. Ancient redwoods, five and six and seven hundred years old, sang praises to the blue and lifting sky. In one place where we stopped, they had gathered themselves into a circle of community, perhaps five or six of them, as though pulling up chairs to tell tales and catch up on centuries now past.

Out of the stillness of the wooded grove, we climbed, up several thousand feet to a visit worth selling stocks to see, up to where I stood above the clouds that beckoned me to walk on them, perhaps south to San Jose or Santa Cruz. Mt. Tamalpais provided a view that stretched from the Carquinez Straits on out beyond what the eye could see but the heart could imagine. The coastline, the city, the bridges, and the bay in splendid union. And the magic carpet of clouds—still beckoning.

I could not help but hear the ancient song of the psalmist, in words even older than the ones from Genesis:

O Lord, our Sovereign,
    how majestic is your name in all the earth!

Tim Tiffany is pastor of First Christian Church in Medford, Oregon.

You have set your glory above the heavens....
When I look at your heavens, the work of your fingers,
  the moon and the stars that you have established;
what are human beings that you are mindful of them,
  mortals that you care for them?
Yet you have made them a little lower than God,
  and crowned them with glory and honor.
You have given them dominion over the works of your hands;
  you have put all things under their feet,
all sheep and oxen,
  and also the beasts of the field,
the birds of the air, and the fish of the sea,
  whatever passes along the paths of the seas.
O Lord, our Sovereign,
  how majestic is your name in all the earth!
            (Psalm 8:1, 3–9)

There is a resounding sense of God's blessing and mighty acts in creation. And along with that, the wonderful reality that *we* are a little lower than the God who creates out of nothing. We are stewards, given dominion over all the works of God's hands. What an incredible wonder!

The first book of our Bible tells us that this magnificent creation was the result of God's ordering hand: In the beginning, "the earth was a formless void and darkness covered the face of the deep" (Genesis 1:2a). Chaos reigned.

So God moved to bring order, moved to put things together in harmonious fashion, separating waters and land, partitioning the darkness of night from the light of day, dreaming up all sorts of vegetation, plants, and fruit. There were stars to craft and seasons to name, days to number off into weeks and months and years; suns and moons to think about and move around like cows and zebras, giraffes and gila monsters; all sorts of wild animals, enough to fill a Barnum & Bailey Circus.

And then God sought mirror images of the very Self of God: "Let us make humankind in our image, according to our likeness; and let them have dominion..." (Genesis 1:26).

Dominion! Right there things began to get out of hand—because when God handed out "dominion," humankind thought God said "domination." And chaos and disorder crept back into the created way of things; and since then, for all time, the push and the pull and the struggle between dominion on the one hand and domination on the other hand has nipped at the heels of the human race and our global home.

We heard words like "Be fruitful and multiply, and fill the earth and subdue it." We heard the word "over"—you shall be over the birds and over the fishes—over and over and over again! Eight times in three verses.

The struggle between dominion and domination has gone on ever since. Some suggest that the biblical text "encourages a sense of human detachment from, and superiority to, nature."

In other words, it's ours! We were given it, we're in charge, we can do with it what we need in order to survive.

Others see this as a false interpretation, believing that it is clear that our text "sets dominion in the context of universal harmony and goodness, in which the human vocation is care and responsibility for nature." (Both quotes are from "Dominion Over Creation" in the supplementary volume of *The Interpreter's Dictionary of the Bible*, p. 247.)

I felt that same tugging even in the splendor of Muir Woods. As we sat on a bridge spanning the little stream, driven to silence by the majestic surroundings, a tour bus arrived. What was vital for them was not silence but the magic of their own voices. And they competed with one another to dominate the conversation. Somehow their laughter and raucous voices were a pollutant at just that moment.

As we looked out on Marin County and beyond from the tip-top of Tam, one could not help but think about the marred realities below, hidden by the distance: shorelines ravaged by droppings from the latest human invasions, bay waters mixed with illegal sickness piped out from plants, air that contained the stuff of our future diseases, and land gone to ruin with the weight of way too much concrete and not enough oxygen-giving greenery.

The newspapers we left back home told of further damages—articles written about the volumes of toxic waste in Contra Costa County alone and the leftover anger and illness from the recent spillage of just such waste, sitting on a side rail in an innocent-looking train container, capable of fear-inducing and paralyzing magic.

And I couldn't help thinking, as I grew hungry, about a recent conversation with an elementary school teacher who had returned from Central America. There she had seen the rain forests bowing before the might of the bulldozer. Why? So that land could be cleared and cows could be fattened to provide the hamburgers you and I had this weekend over the backyard barbeque grills or perhaps at the counter of McDonald's or Burger King.

And she said that old folks she talked with were experiencing new weather, unlike any they had known in sixty or seventy years. Freak of nature? Accident? Or the awful result of mishearing when God said "dominion" and we heard "domination"?

The cynicism of subjugation in our world says, "It's mine to dominate or destroy. I can do anything I want with anything I can lay my hands on." This leads in every aspect of life to every one of us acting as though we were an island unto ourselves, birthing chaos, disorder, and destruction in human global relationships.

The Creation story ends with God's sabbath:

> God now surveys his work and is well pleased. It has come from his hand precisely as he intended it and is therefore very good. The chaos has been effectively restrained and order prevails; the world is furnished and populated, and [hu]mankind has been brought into being to maintain God's created order....The setting is provided for the drama of [humankind]. The account thus presents with soberness and exaltation something of the grandeur of [humanity], the beauty of creation, and [our] joy in the gift of life. (From John Mark's commentary on "Genesis" in *The Interpreter's One-Volume Commentary on the Bible*, p.4.)

Walther Eichrodt, in his book *Theology of the Old Testament* (Vol. II, p. 127) put it another way. We have received, he wrote, "a common universal task. [Humankind] is hereby made the responsible representative of the divine cosmic Lord."

To speak of ecological/theological concerns in a sermon is like trying to wash an elephant in fifteen minutes or so! The field is wide, the viewpoints often diverse and divisive, and we add to the equation a real sense of powerlessness.

What can I do? What difference will it make? Haven't we already made such a mess that there's no getting back to the garden?

Al Gore, in his book *Earth in the Balance*, writes out of a real sense of these questions being spiritual questions. Whether one agrees with where the Vice-President comes out on the issue is not important. What is important is that here is someone writing out of a faith construct. He knows the Genesis passage and the psalmist's writings from a personal journey of faith. In the chapter on "Environmentalism of the Spirit," Gore writes about how we are governed by "a kind of inner ecology that relates perception, emotions, thinking, and choices to forces outside ourselves....But," he continues:

> this ecology now threatens to fall badly out of balance because the cumulative impact of the changes brought by the scientific and technological revolution are potentially devastating to our sense of who we are and what our purpose in life might be....No wonder we have become disconnected from the natural world—indeed, it's remarkable we feel any connection to ourselves. And no wonder we have become resigned to the idea of a world without a future. The engines of distraction are gradually destroying the inner ecology of the human experience. Essential to the ecology is the balance between a belief in the individual and a commitment to the community, between our love for the world and our fear of losing it—the balance, in other words, on which an environmentalism of the spirit depends. (p. 241f.)

So what might it mean for us to begin moving toward an environmentalism of the spirit within this church family? It might begin with a simple acknowledgment by all of us that "*it*" is all connected. The sense of humankind *over against* itself and *over against* the air and the waters and the land is not sense, but nonsense! As Joseph Sittler, Lutheran theologian, commented, "Nature is like a fine piece of cloth; you pull a thread here and it vibrates through the whole fabric" (quoted in *Context*, July 1, 1993). We are a part of that fabric, and it is time for us to discover, or recover, an inner ecology that begins to address our cavalier and careless attitudes about the resources of Mother Earth.

We might begin by being open with one another as this year of exploration unfolds. Being patient when others do not see things the way we see them. Being tender towards all we meet. Taking time to think about the implications of all that we do, every purchase we make. Whatever we do, let us acknowledge right here and right now that we have two major obstacles to overcome in order to reclaim a rightful understanding of dominion.

Those roadblocks are denial and despair. Any realistic hope for the future of the planet must (said Gore in an April 8, 1992, interview in *The Christian Century*) begin by breaking through the denial—the tendency to look away, to divert ourselves, to be entertained: "We must give ourselves permission to experience grief over what has been done to our earth, and what is still going on, but then we have to reject despair as another excuse....People of faith especially must recognize the need for active response" (p. 374).

We live and we move in the power of hope, says Paul in Romans 8. The hope of which Paul writes always recognizes a fundamental unity and harmony of being.

> HOPE believes in imagination.
> HOPE lives in love.
> HOPE never gives up!
>
> Hope is the thing with feathers
> That perches in the soul!
> And sings the tune without the words
> And never stops—at all. (Emily Dickinson)

You and I can change the world—with hope, in hope. Oh, not the WORLD world, but the world we know. The world where we put in gardens and mow lawns, the world where we work and worship. The only world we can change is the one we know. But that will be enough. It will be enough!

$\mathcal{A}$ Sabbath Gift for Stewardship

D. Edward Taylor

This sermon explores the relationship between two culturally offensive ideas: stewardship and Sabbath. The idea of boundaries and identity are alien to the culture that pushes the limits and scoffs at boundaries. But this sermon contains living seeds that can help people discover purpose and stability in life.

Thus the heavens and the earth were finished, and all their multitude. And on the seventh day God finished the work that he had done, and he rested on the seventh day from all the work that he had done. So God blessed the seventh day and hallowed it, because on it God rested from all the work that he had done in creation (Genesis 2:1–3).

During my six days at the Missionaries of Charity children's hospital and orphanage in Port-Au-Prince, I saw many sides of Sister Laeta. One moment she would be barring entrance to a government worker and the next she was inciting children to laughter with a rubber snake. From taking an inventory of supplies she would step to the gate to baptize a child dying in its mother's arms. There was always a group of parents and children at the gate pleading with voices, eyes, and outstretched hands for help. Most of the children suffered from AIDS, tuberculosis, or malnourishment. In this oasis for Haiti's destitute children, Sister Laeta moved compassionately, confidently, and joyfully among the children, the volunteers, and her staff.

This was amazing in light of the physical and emotional demands of parents and children in the world's second poorest

Ed Taylor is director of stewardship for the Church Finance Council, Indianapolis, Indiana.

146

nation. During an afternoon visit, one of the Sisters described a week's routine. Each day began with worship. Specific times of prayer were held during the day. Portions of the day were committed to work with the poorest of the poor in a hospice, wound clinic, and children's hospital. Thursday was a day for household and personal chores, reading, games, writing, and prayer. Sundays were given to worship, prayer, and rest. Daily life moved to the rhythms of work and rest, prayer and play.

Though seemingly worlds apart, that community of faith in Haiti speaks to us of stewardship. The demands and rhythms of their lives speak to us of the contribution of sabbath to faithful Christian stewardship.

Here I speak of stewardship as the care and keeping of creation, a trust from God. Our call, our Christian vocation, is to be stewards of what belongs to God and is entrusted into our care. As individuals and as a community of faith, our trust includes money and possessions, time and abilities, human and nonhuman creation, the good news of Christ and mysteries of God. Our stewardship is characterized by our life in Jesus Christ, who guides us as disciples and fellow servants.

When we look to the book of Genesis and speak of the seven days of creation, we proclaim that God's rest, sabbath, is a vital part of the act of creation. Sabbath is a gift from God that encourages and focuses our stewardship. The gift of sabbath and the call to stewardship are both viewed, by the Christian community, in light of the life, death, and resurrection of Jesus Christ. Observed each week as a time of worship and rest, sabbath helps to provide boundaries for our lives. Within these boundaries we can discover the richness and depth of our Christian stewardship.

We have been among the communities threatened by flood waters. As the river rose, we watched it invade homes and businesses. We witnessed the devastation caused by floods throughout the Midwest and across the United States. Moving beyond the limits of their natural banks, the waters became destructive. Within the limits of the banks, the rivers provided hospitality for commerce, recreation, and wildlife.

Living within the limits of our financial resources calls for difficult but meaningful decisions about what we value. Today's easy credit and increasing allure of lotteries tempts us to live beyond limits. Our stewardship of the earth's resources requires us to live within limits of the nature of soil, water, air, and vegetation. When our consumer orientation moves beyond the limits of our caretaker calling, we are a threat to the earth. Violence on our streets, in our workplaces, and in our households suggest that we have moved beyond the boundaries. As our human relationships move within the boundaries of our Christian discipleship, we affirm the purposes of the household of God.

Sabbath reaffirms limits to our dominion over all the earth. In our worship and rest we are enabled to embrace what God has done and is doing in the world. God's purposes become our purposes. We become partners with God in the ongoing acts of creation. Our partnership in God's purposes is defined by the obedience and servanthood we know in Christ Jesus.

Wendell Berry has written a series of novels that include a character named Mat Feltner. He is a husband, father, grandfather, farmer, neighbor, friend, and steward of the land. In the story called *The Boundary*, Mat Feltner is found late in his life. One afternoon he decides to take a walk. Stepping off the porch of his Kentucky farmhouse, he begins a walk along the boundary of his farm. His labored steps take him across the ridge, along the fence row, and down to the grove. As he walks within the boundary of his farm, he remembers those from whom he inherited the land. His memory joins him to his own father, to his son with whom he repaired the fence, and to neighbors who shared the labor of planting and harvest. Within the boundaries of that portion of land, he knows who he is.

As the church, we discover something of our identity as we move within the boundaries of our biblical roots, our heritage, our shared ministries, our unique resources, and our particular sense of mission. Our sense of belonging to God in Christ becomes increasingly clear.

Sabbath creates a space in time in which we can know who we are. By our rest and worship we join God in looking upon what God has created. In reflection, we know that we belong to God as distinct participants in creation and in the ministry of the church. In sabbath rest we discover who we are and who we have been called to be as disciples of and witnesses to Jesus Christ.

A great pianist was once asked by an ardent admirer: "How do you handle the notes as well as you do?" The artist answered, "The notes I handle no better than many pianists, but the pauses between the notes—ah! that is where the art resides."

The demands and expectations in our daily lives seem unending. This is true for the church community as well as for the individual. There are always meals to prepare, classes to teach, music to rehearse, food to deliver, clothing to collect, offerings to promote and interpret, persons to visit, services to prepare. Our physical, emotional, and spiritual energies are drawn upon in home, business, school, and church.

In our sabbath rest, we are joined to God's liberating power. We are set free from the need to control, to do all things, to accomplish. Sabbath challenges our sense of urgency, striving, grasping, collecting, with a call to trust in God's creative Spirit. In our freedom to be God's people in Jesus Christ, we are led to confidence, compassion, and joy as the way of living the good news in a demanding world.

*L*IVING TO GIVE – GIVING TO LIVE

Larry Paul Jones

> *This sermon is an excellent example of the weaving of ancient and modern. It embodies the relationship of worshipful stewardship. Preparation opens one to wholeness. Giving opens one to life. We need this realistic presentation of a widow at worship.*

Mark 12:38–44

The eve of their arrival at the temple meant nothing special to the scribes, wealthy merchants, and prominent members of the community. They came to the temple regularly and were familiar with the pomp, circumstance, splendor, and procedures of the rites and rituals. They had their servants make sure that the pleats on their robes were neatly folded and that the tassels designating their standing were still in place. They wanted to look impressive as they paraded through the outer courtyards into the court of Israel. Some probably sent couriers to invite one of the priestly families to dine with them after the morning sacrifices. That wouldn't hurt their standing. It might even help land a wealthy husband for one of their daughters or a bride with a large dowry for one of their sons. They routinely checked the ornate bags in which they carried their temple offerings to make sure that they had the proper coins and that the amount was sufficient for persons of their rank. They did this all the time. There was nothing extraordinary or unusual about it.

Across town, in a dimly lit, immaculately swept hovel, all thoughts and energies were directed toward the next day. The widow meticulously cleaned her threadbare shawl, pensively

Larry Paul Jones is professor of homiletics at Lexington Theological Seminary in Lexington, Kentucky.

150

wondered whether she would have the stamina to make her way through the crowd of worshipers, and checked for the hundredth time the faded cloth in which she had tied her temple offering. Earlier that week she had bargained hard with the baker to purchase a loaf of bread and still have something left for the temple, but she had managed. After all, she couldn't approach the house of God empty-handed. She closed her eyes and smiled. She could almost see the stately columns of the temple, hear the bleating of sheep, and smell the pungent odor of the sacrifices.

At the moment, she lived to give her offering to God. Widows like her, rulers like Herod, and haughty troops like the Romans would come and go. As long as Israel remained faithful, the temple and the blessings of God found there would endure forever. Her means were modest. She had lost her husband, her children, and many of her friends. If something did not happen soon, she would lose even the tumble-down walls and roof around her. But she lived to give her offering to God. She wanted to tell God, "I'm thankful I still have you."

Out of the large crowd of worshipers, she was the one Jesus noticed. Of her Jesus said, "Truly I tell you, this poor widow has put in more than all those who are contributing to the treasury. For all of them have contributed out of their abundance; but she out of her poverty has put in everything she had" (Mark 12:43–44). He saw that she lived to give.

That's enough storytelling. Now for some meddling. About what did we think last night? Surely none of us were vain or shallow enough to sit up wondering how others would respond to our apparel, appearance, or participation in worship. (Were we?) But as we went about our Saturday routine, did we give any thought at all to worship? If we did, what were those thoughts? Did we look forward to offering praises to God, or did we hope to hear a stirring anthem? Did we take time to notice whether anyone we know could use an invitation or a ride to church, or did we hope the service would end early enough not to interfere with our plans? Did we give any thought to our regular offering or to special needs that might have arisen in the congregation, the community, or the denomination, or did we write the check without pausing, simply out of habit?

As we worship today, will Jesus notice what we have to offer? Will he be able to say of us, "They live to give"?

Living to give seems contrary to our way of life. We define success in terms of what can be taken from life, not in terms of what can be given. That holds as true in the church as it does in the marketplace.

Following the advice of trained consultants (Who can do anything today without first hiring a consultant?), we market churches much as we market consumer goods. We focus on what the church has to offer. Some of us offer to save others from hell. We invite people to come to church so they can gain salvation. There is nothing wrong with focusing on eternal salvation, but is that all there is to being a part of the church?

Others of us take a more earthly approach. We build gymnasia and racquetball courts, offer aerobic classes and jazzercizes, and provide child-care services and nutrition classes. Consultants assure us that congregations that offer these and other services are the most attractive. There is nothing wrong with such programs and services, but they all focus on the individual and what that individual can receive from the church. Is that all there is to being a part of the church?

Jesus took a different approach. He called his initial followers to be "fishers of people." He called them into ministry. He asked them to do something: to tend sheep, to heal the sick, to feed the hungry, to clothe the naked, to visit the imprisoned, and to preach good news. He focused on services to render, not on goods to receive. Jesus praised a poor widow who placed all she had in the temple treasury. He praised her because she was more interested in taking part in God's presence than in buying some product God or the temple had to offer.

Mark doesn't say what happened in the temple after the widow made her offering. A few people probably snickered and taunted her. Some may have aimed disapproving glances in her direction. Many may simply have turned away to keep from shaming her.

For her part, her eyes may have avoided the crowd. Her shoulders may have been as stooped when she left the temple as they were when she came. But when she returned home there surely was energy in her step and a glow in her heart. Unlike so many of the scribes, wealthy merchants, and prominent members of the community, she left that morning knowing she had participated in worship and in ministry generously, intentionally, and with integrity. She had given her all. She had held back nothing. Ironically, she who gave away everything she had returned home more full than those who had given only a part. Her giving made her alive.

Sometimes we are surprised by grace in spite of ourselves. Sometimes the planning and execution by others leads to rich experiences of worship from which we leave feeling filled. But what might happen if we gave our all? If we entered the sanctuary intending and planning to offer our praises to God in song, just how powerfully might the Spirit move in among us! If we came intending and planning to pray, how awesome might be our silences! If we honestly dedicated the best of our talents and time to working together and to building community, how filled and fulfilled might our lives become! If we truly committed our financial and physical resources to ministry in the name of Jesus the Christ, how many people in our country and beyond might have their lives changed by the love and grace of God? Giving brings faith to life.

Jesus noticed the widow who gave everything she had. That act does not romanticize poverty. There is nothing sacred about being hungry, cold, homeless, or powerless. The presence of the poor illustrates the need for church and its mission. But sometimes people who live near the edge of existence see things more clearly than those of us who have plenty. They see without impairment what is essential.

The widow praised by Jesus knew she had nothing and no one on whom to rely but God. Her gift told God, "I have nothing more to offer. Take and use me."

We have much more to offer than that poor widow, but we are not that different from her. People like us, leaders like ours, and problems like those which face us come and go. God endures forever. Living means giving no less than our very selves to God. Giving no less than our very selves to God means coming truly alive.

Think about it. Pray about it. For the love of God, do something about it.

*Y*OUR LIFE IS REQUIRED OF YOU

Timothy L. Carson

> *Some sermons are compex and difficult to follow.*
> *Therefore, they are difficult to live. However, this sermon*
> *is straightforward and to the point. Basic illustrations*
> *come from the community of faith and, thus, connect*
> *people to real memory. The encouragement of mentors in*
> *spiritual growth and living is something that must be*
> *nurtured in congregational life. Too much modern*
> *advice to accumulate works against the assumption of*
> *this sermon that people can grow.*

Luke 12:13–21

I was only out of seminary for a short time, pastoring my first church, when I encountered two people who taught me valuable lessons. They were not all that unusual—much like you and me. Yet, on the other hand, they were unique.

The first was an elderly man who had developed bone cancer. Before the later and more critical phases of his illness, he spent much time at home, and in particular resting on a cot he set up in the breezeway between the house and the garage. As he lay there, he would look up at his vast collection of tools on the peg board and think about them. He told me, "I'd look up at a tool—one that used to seem so important, one I just had to have—and I would think to myself, 'You know, it really doesn't mean anything. It's not that important.'" And he would look at those tools, taking a sort of inventory, I suppose, not only of the tools but of life and of what matters, and how different things looked from his new perspective. It was a kind of conversion experience for him, the dawning of a whole new awareness occasioned by his own mortality.

The second person was a woman in the church who was a compulsive collector. I suppose it bordered on being an addiction.

Tim Carson is senior pastor of Webster Groves Christian Church in St. Louis, Missouri. He and his wife Kathy are the co-authors of *So You're Thinking About Contemporary Worship* (Chalice Press).

One can only suspect the vacancies in her life that prompted her to gather all manner of things to fill the empty spaces, but that is what she did. Her home became a sort of warehouse. One whole bedroom was outfitted with commercial-type clothes racks to hold all the clothes she bought, many of which were never worn.

Her dining room could no longer be used to eat in. It was filled with all manner of glass and porcelain pieces. There was barely room to sit anywhere because the things she had obtained demanded most of the space. The shopkeepers in town smiled when they saw her coming. Her husband, who knew her best and loved her most, just shrugged.

I conducted the funerals of both of these wonderful and active church people, later to watch as many of those possessions were first given away to family and friends and the remainder sold at auction on their front lawns. In a dramatic way the parable of this morning came to life.

Once upon a time, Jesus said, there was a rich man who accumulated so much that he built more and more barns to store it all. Then he said to himself in a self-satisfied way, "Now sit back, enjoy the fruits of your labors, enjoy the good life." Just about the time those words came out of his mouth, the leg of his lawn chair gave way, he tumbled down the terrace of his manicured lawn, fell off a deck, plunged into the hot tub, and drowned. A terrible scene.

And the word of God suddenly came to him: "Fool! This very night your life is demanded of you. And all these things with which you've surrounded yourself—to whom will they belong now?" The parable concludes with a saying: So it is for those who store up treasures for themselves but are not rich toward God.

What are we building? More barns to house more things in the mad and compulsive race to possess? The achievement of some status or importance? What are we building?

Not too long ago I observed what is probably an urban parable. Someone was driving to work one morning, heading downtown, talking on the car phone. And on top of the car sat one of those no-spill coffee mugs with the broad base coated with foam rubber. It looked like a kind of emergency light atop the car, as though at any moment the coffee mug might start flashing, warning others to get out of the way as he sped to attend to some urgent matter. This guy hadn't the foggiest idea why fellow commuters continued to smirk at him. You are so harried, so scattered, you even leave your coffee on the roof of your car. It's something I could do just as easily.

What kind of a life are we building, and for what? What are we missing and sacrificing to do so? Is the workaholic, obsessed rat race worth it? And could it be that all this merely serves as a substitute for something else that really matters?

Jesus' parable tells us that our lives may be required of us at any time, which causes us to think about right now in ultimate terms, and the question is: What are we building? In the mad race to succeed, to accumulate, to surround ourselves with the accouterments of the good life, *are we building our lives around God?*

For the new Christian, the person new to faith, this may be a new idea—building our lives around God. Before God is in the picture, life is built around everything else. But for the long-term Christian, the Christian who has fallen into a rut, the nominal Christian, the Christian who has just temporarily lost his or her way, it may be more a matter of *forgetfulness.*

Recently I heard about a little girl with a new baby brother. The little girl told her parents that she wanted some time to be alone with the new baby. The parents were a little hesitant at first; what could she possibly be up to? They were aware of the possibilities of sibling rivalry. Finally they agreed but left the room monitor on to listen. Once alone, the small girl, to her parents' surprise, urgently asked the baby, "Please, won't you tell me about God? I'm beginning to forget."

It is easy to forget, and we who are Christians often become afflicted with a kind of spiritual amnesia, as we forget who we are and whose we are. In that state of forgetfulness, we end up building our lives around everything but God.

This relates directly to the interior logic of the commandment to remember the sabbath to keep it holy. Christians worship regularly not only because we need to praise our God in the presence of other spiritual pilgrims, but also as a medicine against forgetfulness. In the singing of the hymns, the reading of scripture, prayer, proclamation of the faith, baptism, the Lord's supper, we are reminded of who we are, for what we shall live, and around whom we shall build our lives. We gather regularly, lest we forget.

What are you building your life around? Another way to put the question is to ask, "How do you spend your time? How do you give your money? How do you use your God-given talents?" All in all, what percentage of this is built around God?

The answer to these practical questions will tell the real story of the commitments of your life. Most certainly it tells the real story to your children. Talk as you will about being a

Christian, parents, but remember: Your children are watching, and your example tells the true story.

As a congregation, too, we must ask the same question: Are we building our life around God? In the church it is easy to build the congregation's life around *substitutes* for God that appear religious. If this becomes the case, the church ironically becomes a barrier to God. If the community of faith becomes just another social club where people who are alike gather to enjoy one another's company, or a place where the status quo is more honored than the pursuit of the will of God, or where the consumeristic mentality of meeting my wants and needs becomes more important than a sense of mission, we can be most certain we are building on the wrong foundation, on the shifting sand of that which cannot last.

On the other hand, if we have a sense of the Spirit of God leading us to dynamic worship that reaches to many people—to new forms of Christian education for all ages; to lay-centered ministries of Christian caring; to an enlarged sense of congregational mission, such our our new mission, The Olive Branch, for homeless, pregnant teens in St. Louis; to the development of intentional and intimate small groups where Christian community, scripture study, and prayer may be fostered; to the compassionate and committed use of our money now and after our deaths for the continuing mission of the church; to a sense of sharing our talents in the church for the glory of God—then we can begin to know that we are building our life around God.

Professors from the Harvard University School of Education once arranged a visit to a school and said to all the teachers, "We are going to go into your classrooms and we're going to be giving a test to be called the Harvard Test of Intellectual Spurts. It is going to measure which kids in your classrooms are going to grow intellectually during the year that they're in your class. And it will pick them out. It never fails. We'll be able to tell you, and think of what a help this will be."

So they went in and they administered some old obsolete IQ tests, collected them—and threw them in the trash. Then they went to the class roster and chose five names at random. They sat down with the teacher. They said, "These five children are going to spurt this semester."

The teachers were always dumbfounded because the list of pupils who would spurt was always a very mixed one—children with vastly different abilities and potentials. "Nevertheless, the Harvard Test of Intellectual Spurts never fails," said the experts. And do you know what happened? Of course you do. Every name they had put on that list spurted all over the place. They had liberated the power of expectation.

Today I think it would be a good idea to administer our own test. It is called the *Webster Groves Christian Church Test of Spiritual Spurts*. But I can tell you now, even before administering the test, that you all will be identified for a spiritual spurt. And I can tell you why this test is totally reliable: It is because you are baptized. You belong to Christ, and your life is built around him. And God is leading you beyond your amnesia into being the person you were created to be from before the beginning of time.

This very day, and every day, your life is demanded of you. Are you frantically building new barns? Or are you building your life around God?

$\mathcal{J}$OYFUL GIVING

David P. Polk

This sermon includes an excellent parable that can be used in the preaching of many sermons on stewardship. Variable responses to giving are helpful in the congregation seeking to understand its own attitude about resources and sharing. There are fresh thoughts here for preaching about the life that finds joy in giving.

2 Corinthians 9:6–15

In a strange land and a strange time, a decree went out to all the people from the One In Charge. The decree was prominently posted and publicly proclaimed so that all became aware of it. The decree consisted of three simple words: GIVING IS FORBIDDEN!

At first, great rejoicing was heard throughout the land. Many felt an enormous burden had been wonderfully lifted from their shoulders. They began to calculate how much happier they would surely be if they could now spend all their income and all their time on themselves and on their own needs and pleasures.

And then, strange things began to happen in this strange land and strange time. A little boy forgot the decree and picked a bouquet of flowers to give to his mother. But his mother was forbidden to accept them, and the flowers wound up in the trash can. A passing motorist saw a battered victim of highway robbers lying in a ditch by the road. She pulled alongside him to help, then thought better of it. How can I help him, she said to herself, since he obviously has nothing left with which to repay me? And the motorist drove away, sadly.

David Polk is editor of Chalice Press and vice president of Christian Board of Publication in St. Louis, Missouri. He has taught classes on stewardship at Brite Divinity School, Texas Christian University. This sermon appeared previously in the *Journal of Stewardship* (Vol. 47, 1995).

But strangest of all were the experiences of those who rejoiced so enthusiastically when the burden of giving had been taken from them. They now found themselves no better off than before. That slim amount of income which they had been giving away was disappearing into an extra suit of clothes and more meals in fine restaurants and a new home computer and a trip to an exotic land. But none of this made anyone any happier. There were still so many things just barely beyond reach.

A delegation was sent to the One In Charge. "We appreciate your intentions," said the spokesperson, "in lifting from us the burden of giving. But, alas, now we're doubly miserable. Not only are we frustrated that we never seem to have enough, but we've also been stripped of the joy that comes in sharing ourselves with another. Please take back your decree. We think we've learned the lesson that giving is not a burden but a joy. Give back to us our joy!"

So it came to be, in this land and time of great strangeness. And did they give happily ever after? The story provides no answer—because the only answer possible is the one that we insert into it. Do *we* "give happily ever after"? Is there a kind of giving that is really joyful—enriching to the giver and not just to the one who receives the gift? That's a truly important question.

To explore that, I want to take you on a journey into one of Paul's letters to the church in Corinth. Hard times had befallen the faithful in Jerusalem. One of the purposes of Paul's second Corinthian letter was to urge the church in Corinth to participate in an offering that he was collecting on behalf of those who were in dire straits down south. The entire eighth and ninth chapters of the letter are focused on encouraging the Corinthian Christians to discover their capacity to respond generously to this special appeal.

As Paul is wrapping up his remarks, he offers an interesting observation: "God loves a cheerful giver." Now take a moment and consider the quartet of possible alternatives. In addition to joyful givers there might be joyless givers. And then there are joyful non-givers to consider, as well as joyless non-givers. Let's examine those four options and see if any of these combinations ring more true than others, and then inquire about the scope of God's love.

I think the least realistic of the four is the notion of the "joyful non-giver." Certainly, as we receive and spend resources with which our lives are sustained, there are times when we experience the feeling reflected in the story of The Decree: "Oh, if only there weren't so many needs to which my giving is called to respond, if only God did not impose the burden on me to share a portion of what I worked very hard to get and now am entitled to, then I would be truly happy with what I can do with those resources." I believe that is a false prospect, as the story suggests. Life lived in such a way is the very opposite of fullness and meaning and joy. At the center is a void.

On the other hand, "joyless non-giving" is a real option. There is hardly a more forlorn person imaginable than Scrooge before his conversion. The trio of specters brings him face-to-face with the joylessness of a rich but impoverished life in which he has turned away from all those who might benefit from his self-giving. You know, it's a shame that the name "Scrooge" denotes a tight-fisted miser, when the whole power and beauty of Charles Dickens' *A Christmas Carol* is the transformation that came when Ebenezer Scrooge threw open the windows of his soul that Christmas morning and began to experience the enrichment that came from sharing his life with others. Joy-less non-giving came to be seen as a prison from which he had been wonderfully set free.

But what about "joyless giving"? Paul touches on that in his letter, reminding his readers that we are offered a challenge to give but invited to make our own free response, not feeling under compulsion (9:7). Giving from a sense of being compelled, giving that is begrudging, is joyless giving. It is the sort of gift we make while wishing we didn't "have to," the kind of giving that is really paltry in spirit, whatever the amount, because there is no sense of rejoicing that underlies it.

So Paul invites us to discover an attitude of giving in which the very act fills us with a sense of the fullness of the life available to us as a gift from God. We are invited, in fact, to discover something I want to call "Scroogian giving"—giving like Scrooge's *after* his Christmas-night conversion, giving characterized by a joy in sharing. And we are informed that such a giver is the one whom God loves.

But there is still more to be unpacked here. Paul knew of a version of Proverbs 22:8 in his Greek translation known as the *Septuagint*. You won't find it in your Bible because it's not in the original Hebrew; the translators added it. It reads: "God blesses a cheerful and giving person." The meaning is quite clear: God rewards those whose attitude in giving is one of joy. Is Paul saying, then, that God rewards the joyful giver with a bestowing of divine love?

Let's not tread that path too quickly. Jesus—and Paul as well—strongly emphasized the fact that God's love for us does not depend on us. God's love depends on God. God's love is freely given. We don't earn God's love—which is precisely what "grace" means. God sustains us lovingly. God empowers us to live in God's love.

So the love of God is not the reward that you are to expect from an outpouring of your heart and pocketbook. God's love is the *enabling* that undergirds our actions, because our actions are none other than responses to a gift from God that is extravagant and unceasing. Therefore, I dare to insist that God loves the joyless giver too. God loves the begrudging giver. God even loves the non-giver—but less effectively, because it is *in* our joyous giving that the love of God comes to be manifested *through* us. And the power that God is offering us shines forth precisely in those circumstances.

The next verse in this passage is a blockbuster. There comes a promise—a very full promise, one that we can easily misunderstand if we're not careful. It is the promise of material well-being: "And God has the power to provide for you every benefit in abundance, that in every way having everything you need, you may abound in every good work."

The Greek word that Paul uses here for abundance is *autarkeia*. Within the Hellenistic culture of which he was a part, it had a vivid meaning: "material self-sufficiency that renders you dependent on no one." It sounds like a nice goal, doesn't it? If only I had enough so that I didn't have to worry about anyone else's actions toward me—my boss, the government, my creditors. If only I were completely and independently self-sufficient. That's what the word meant. *Autarkeia* meant being an island unto myself. No one can mess with my island.

But Paul takes the word and turns it upside down, which is what makes it so fascinating. Paul says: God has power to provide for you every benefit in abundance, all that you need, *autarkeia*. In Paul's twist, the concept of material well-being is the very opposite of being self-contained; it is the notion of being *in relationship* with God on whom our good fortune depends.

And then Paul takes it one enormous step further. The self-sufficiency that God grants us is there for a purpose. And the purpose is as easily misunderstood as the promise. Even the NRSV leaves the mistake in verse eleven uncorrected: "You *will be* enriched in every way for your great generosity." How many bad stewardship sermons have been based on that mistranslation! How much idolatrous championing of a self-ish, materialistic Christianity is trumpeted from this vantage point! But the original Greek conveyed an entirely different message: *It's in the present tense!* You *are* enriched in every way for your great generosity.

That's why this sermon is using the Anchor Bible translation of 2 Corinthians, which renders the meaning correctly: "In everything *being enriched* for all generosity..." God does not promise that we will be enriched as we give. *We are already enriched.* All of us. The *purpose* is so that we are able to manifest greater generosity in our relationships with others, leading to an outpouring of thanksgiving to God. The sufficiency is not something belonging to individuals. It is the way God has constituted planet Earth. The sufficiency, *autarkeia,* is communal. The enrichment is experienced precisely when we are living faithfully in an ever-widening circle of sharing God's bounty.

So why is it so hard to experience that kind of joyful giving, sustained by God's love, enabled and empowered by God? To answer that, we need to confront Jesus' reminder in the Sermon on the Mount: "You cannot serve God and mammon" (Matthew 6:24, RSV). That cuts deep because it names the dilemma we experience. It is not simply a matter of attitude, but something far more insidious. Jesus identified it as *enslavement*. We can be a slave to mammon (wealth) or a servant of God, but not both. "No one can serve two masters."

But the good news is no less than an announcement of liberation: God breaks the chains of bondage. God breaks the chains of bondage to isolation and opens us up to be in community. God offers to us the freedom from bondage to materialism. And that involves nothing less than *conversion* on our part. Stewardship is the material expression of our faithfulness to God, the outward sign of an inward *metanoia* or *conversion*.

Often we find ourselves trying to *do* stewardship a little better, but we're still trapped in enslavement to materialism. My good friend Rhodes Thompson has defined materialism not as "the worship of what we have" but "the worship of what we don't have—but will mortgage everything to get!" I like that. He goes on to suggest that we image our income and possessions as constituting a circle of varying size. Our unhappiness stems from living always at the edge of that circle, peering out over the boundary and thinking to ourselves, "If only I had just this little bit more, if only my circle were just a little bit larger—then I could be truly happy." But the curse is that no matter how much the circle expands, we always find ourselves living again at the new edge, still yearning for yet one more increase. That is enslavement to mammon, becoming entrapped by one's possessions and craving for yet more.

Joy comes not from expanding the circle, beyond the scope of genuine need. Joy comes when we experience the power that sets us free to begin living out of the bounty of what we have rather than in the misery of what we don't have. My hope is that each one of us may experience the gift of empowerment that enables us to break out of the chains of bondage to mammon and discover the treasure of joyful living that manifests itself in joyful giving.